Cooking with Smitty's Mom

Cooking with Smitty's Mom

Barbara Smith and Michael W. Smith

A
JANET
THOMA
BOOK

THOMAS NELSON PUBLISHERS
Nashville

Published in Nashville, Tennessee, by Thomas Nelson, Inc.

Library of Congress Cataloging–in–Publication Data

Smith, Barbara.
    Cooking with Smitty's mom / Barbara Smith and Michael W. Smith.
       p. cm.
    ISBN 0-7852-6918-5 (pbk.)
    1. Cookery. I. Smith, Michael W. (Michael Whitaker) II. Title.
TX714.S5885 1999
641.5—dc21

99–25998
CIP

Printed in the United States of America
1 2 3 4 5 6 7 8 HG 04 03 02 01 00 99

This book is dedicated to
my family for their love and support
and to all the wonderful people
God has allowed to be a part of my life.

Contents

Michael arrives at his fortieth birthday party at Green's Grocery.

Introduction

October 7, 1997—Smitty's fortieth birthday. That milestone had to be marked, and Michael's wife, Debbie, and I were determined to do so. We both checked out possible sites for the great event and finally found a little place, Green's Grocery, in Leiper's Fork, about ten miles outside of Franklin, Tennessee, where we all live. Green's Grocery is owned by Aubrey Preston, who first opened the renovated grocery store as a restaurant. There is a lot of history there.

In its early years many famous artists performed there: Amy Grant, Michael McDonald, Vince Gill, Wynonna, Delbert McClinton, Larry Carlton. Also many people came as guests, like Faith Hill and Tim McGraw. Later Aubrey decided to close Green's Grocery as a restaurant and just rent it on weekends for special functions.

Lots of memorabilia hang on the walls of the main room: unique old guitars, "outsider art," and artifacts from the old grocery store. Outside is a big yard with picnic tables. This setting was perfect for the many children: Michael's own five: Ryan, Whitney, Tyler, Anna, and Emily; our daughter Kimberly's two: Mary Claire and Caroline; and all those other children who form our extended family and friends circle.

Debbie and a neighbor, Duane Ward, decided they would get Michael to the party in a unique way. They blindfolded Michael, guided him onto a rented bus, which held the whole family, and drove to Leiper's Fork. They didn't take the blindfold off until he walked into the main room. Everybody was there. Three hundred people, in fact.

It was a special evening. We got out all the pictures from Michael's childhood and career, and old videos of Michael with lots of different hairstyles. Chris Harris, a friend who used to play in the band with Michael, planned the whole program. Amy Grant sang and spoke. Franklin Graham flew in from North Carolina. (Michael sings at many of his crusades and has accompanied him to Bosnia and other war-torn countries to distribute shoe boxes of presents for children.) Franklin had Dennis Agajanian with him, and Dennis sang. The group Avalon sang, and Paul Overstreet also sang.

Since I had been a professional caterer for thirteen years, I was in charge of the food. We had Layered Salad (page 89), Fresh Fruit (page 47), Sesame

Avalon entertains the guests
at Michael's party.

Green's Grocery in
Leiper's Fork

Michael
reminisces
during the
festivities.

Chicken (page 133), baked ham, Green Beans (page 116), Sour Cream Potatoes (page 117), Loaf Bread (page 74), and Whipped Butter (page 68), accompanied by iced tea and soft drinks. And of course, birthday cakes.

The buffet was served in an enclosed porch, but people ate both inside and out. Most of the children stayed outside the entire time. We had prepared hot dogs and special things for them, but they also ate the food on the buffet.

Michael's party is the one time I ran out of food (just sesame chicken and sour cream potatoes), since we had invited 250 people and 300 showed up. (As my husband, Paul, says, "Nobody RSVPs in Nashville.") We had plenty of everything else, because we started cutting the servings. I had baked and frozen thirty loaves of bread over a period of weeks, so we didn't run out of bread.

That one time taught me that I would rather have leftovers than run out. Now I always take too much food to any occasion. Debbie's dad just loves that because he gets to take the leftover bread home! We have family dinners frequently (almost every month); it is always someone's birthday.

I believe that celebrations of this kind are great opportunities for us to show our friends and loved ones how much they mean to us through the service of good food.

Food and the Family

Unfortunately, in our fast-paced society, family dinners and home-cooked meals are becoming more and more rare. I recently heard someone say that their idea of a sit-down family dinner was when they picked up their food at the drive-through window of McDonald's. Now, I realize that's a lighthearted exaggeration, but there's usually a kernel of truth at the core of most jokes.

People just don't do a lot of cooking anymore. There's a quip about Fieldstone Farms, our housing development here in Franklin: it has nice homes but no kitchens. That's another exaggeration, but again it has a kernel of truth. We heard a story about one couple (both of them worked) who bought a home here. They splurged for all the upgrades, particularly in the kitchen. They lived there two years and decided to sell their home. It's said that they had yet to cook in that fancy kitchen!

Recently I saw an article in our local paper about a chef who started an unusual business; he comes into your home for a day and prepares just what you want. For $200 he cooks approximately ten meals. The lady who hired him said, "That will take care of my family for a month."

I know we are living in a fast-paced society, but I think we need to nurture our families by cooking for them ourselves when possible and making family meals a special time. When Michael and Kimberly were growing up, I always tried to make mealtime a family event. I think that's because I missed the feeling of a close-knit family when I was young.

Unfortunately, I didn't grow up in a Christian home. My mom left our family when I was six years old. My dad worked out of town; therefore he could not be home as he would have liked. He had to ask extended family members to help him. I went to live with my great-grandmother, my brother lived with my grandmother, and my two sisters lived with two of my aunts. When my great-grandmother died, I went to live with my grandmother.

In 1947 my dad remarried, and we all moved to West Virginia to live with he and my stepmother. She was Italian and was a wonderful cook; she always prepared at least twenty dishes for every holiday meal. In the middle of the feast, she would usually say, "Oh, I left the potato salad in the refrigerator downstairs." I learned much of what I know about cooking from her and my grandmother.

Once I was married and blessed with a wonderful husband and two children, I wanted to create a real sense of family and continuity. I think family time is really important, especially mealtimes. I tried to keep our meals simple and wholesome. Small children often do not like spicy food. I didn't force Michael and Kimberly to eat foods they didn't like. Forcing children to eat often adds tension to mealtime. Most doctors say that children will get the foods they need over a period of time. (To see how I dealt with Michael, who didn't like vegetables, see the introduction to the Vegetables section, page 111.)

I always tried to avoid controversial topics at mealtime. That's not a time to talk about how late a child can stay out or to discuss what the children did wrong that day. For me the most meaningful way to bring peace to a meal is to begin with a blessing. When Michael and Kimberly were little, we held hands and they said the simple grace, "God is great, God is good, and we thank Him for our food."

Paul and I made every effort to create an environment in our home that would encourage Michael and Kimberly to invite their friends over. In fact, I used to joke: "I'm never sure whom I will find sleeping on the living room floor when I get up in the morning." That's because the kids' friends loved hanging out at our house. Michael always said, "Mom, you have the ultimate servant's heart. You are always making something good to eat for whoever happens to pass through."

Now, Paul and I really had a hidden agenda. It was a great way for us to make sure we knew where Michael and Kimberly were. If they were hanging out with friends who wanted to be at our home, we rarely had to worry about them. When Michael looks back on those days, he says, "I now realize what an incredible blessing it was to grow up in a home where love was abundant."

Emilie Barnes calls this a "welcome home" lifestyle in her book, *The Spirit of Loveliness* (Harvest House, 1992). She tells about her early married years when she and her husband had very little financially, but were still working to create a lifestyle that said "welcome" to themselves and everyone around them. I believe, as Emilie does, that we all need a spiritual center, a place where we belong. To me, home should be a place where we can unwind, regroup, and get in touch with who we truly are. Only then can we reach out to share with others.

Derek Jones (who is still helping us as he did way back in 1990) and Don Donahue, president of Rocketown Records, assist us in catering Michael's birthday party.

All that this requires is a willing spirit—a determination to make room in our lives, schedules, and budgets for what comforts us and enriches our souls. Most of all, as Emilie says, it requires an "I can" attitude, a confidence that we have something to share and the ability to share it.

Paul and I enjoy practicing a welcome-home lifestyle for ourselves, our neighbors, and our friends, and we are thankful that both Kimberly and Michael do the same.

I spend lots of time in prayer before a big event like Michael's birthday party. Despite the fact that I've catered since 1979 for as many as five hundred people at a time, I still get nervous, especially when I have to transport food to another location. I ask God to watch over me, to give me a keen mind, and to help me remember all the details. I'm really asking for an overall covering of His Spirit and that He will see me through the event.

My friend Betty Bingham and I both loved to cook. We would occasionally help with the cooking at our church (First Baptist Church of Kenova, West Virginia), where we had many dear friends. One of those dear friends, Simp Griffith, told us one day that he and his wife, Ruth, were going to celebrate their fiftieth wedding anniversary and wondered if we would consider catering their celebration.

We had never catered anything in our lives, and the Griffiths invited four hundred people. Talk about panic! We worked for a month. We did hors d'oeuvres for that event, our first venture into catering: Fresh Fruit (page 47), Millionaire Tarts (page 188), Meringue Shells (page 193) with strawberries, Cream Puffs (page 191), and Strawberry Punch (page 35).

Soon we began to do small events at local churches. We often fixed Baked Steak (page 144), which became a favorite. At first we did events for twenty-five people or so. Then the size and the frequency of the events began to multiply. Without any advertising the word just spread.

We called our business "The Catering Carte," and we did social events for two banks in West Virginia, one in Huntington and the other in Ceredo. We hired two young women and a couple of college boys, Derek Jones and Andrew Scites, to serve. (Derek is now director of Media Relations and Promotions for Michael's record label, Rocketown Records.) Then Paul and Betty's husband, Jack, carried the food from our homes to the event.

One of the banks sponsored a travel group and occasionally had dinners or luncheons for them. If the event started at 6:30 P.M., they were always there at 6:00.

This made last-minute preparation really difficult, since we had to wait until business hours were over before we could begin. Then the bank staff had to move quickly to clear the lobby and set up the tables so that we could set and decorate them. The events became so popular that people began arriving early and sitting down before we could even get the tables set. Every seat was taken at least a half hour before the dinner was supposed to begin.

Normally we prepared two desserts, and we would have the boys, Andrew and Derek, alternate the desserts, like pecan pie and cheesecake, when they served.

One evening Andrew came back and said, "Barbara, I can't get rid of this pecan pie. They all want cheesecake. Every time I set one down, they move it around."

Paul said, "Go out there and tell them it's bourbon pecan pie." (That was true, but I didn't advertise it.) In a few minutes Andrew came back and said, "Barbara, I can't get rid of the cheesecake!"

Despite all the hard work, "The Catering Carte" was a lot of fun.

Sadly, Betty was diagnosed with bone cancer in 1988, and her work was very limited for the next four years before she died. In 1993 I had a hip replacement, so our business ended then. If I were younger, I would love to own a tea room because I enjoy preparing lunch and hors d'oeuvres.

One big party here in Nashville, the launch of Michael's *Live the Life* album, led to this book.

Live the Life Event

When Michael released this album, he and his management company decided to bring in some of the top DJs from all over the United States. Michael asked, "Mom, would you like to cook dinner?" Then just in case I'd feel pressured to do so, he added, "You don't have to if it's going to be too much. We can get it catered."

Since I enjoy being a part of Michael's career in this way, I said yes to his request. The twenty DJs first attended a golf outing at Legends Country Club. Then they came to Michael's house for dinner. When they first arrived, they immediately came into the kitchen and introduced themselves. At that moment I knew it was going to be a great evening! They were very personable!

I served Sesame Chicken (page 133) and Eye of Round Roast with mushroom gravy (page 145). We had Green Beans (page 116), Spinach Casserole (page 122), Stir-Fried Zucchini Squash (page 115), and potato salad (not my choice, but because the lady from Zomba Records in New York requested it). We also had Layered Salad (page 89), Cloverleaf Rolls (page 74), Dilly Bread (page 78), Cheesecake (page 181), Coconut Cream Pie (page 159), Chocolate Cream Pie (page 165), and Chocolate Cake with White Frosting (page 169).

I have cooked for so many people through the years, but these DJs were some of the dearest. Everyone came back for seconds, recipes for their wives or moms, and were very complimentary of the food. (These DJs travel all the time, so they rarely get a home-cooked meal.) Paul and I were overwhelmed by their kindness.

The launch event was a great success, and that's really where this cookbook was born. As Chaz Corzine, Michael's manager, and I were discussing the evening, he said, "You should write a cookbook."

"Well, Chaz, what do I do?" I jokingly responded, and from that brief conversation Chaz pursued the idea. He felt that other women would be interested in my recipes and philosophy of cooking. His wife, Deaver, and

Debbie suggested including a grocery list and pantry (staples) checklist to make the recipes more user-friendly.

It's always more difficult when I cook food at home and transport it to another location. I usually put the food in oblong casserole dishes. Then I transport the hot foods in large thermos coolers because they keep things cold or hot. I layer the dishes and put wire cooling racks in between them. Finally, I put thawed bread on top. (When I make bread, I slice it as soon as it cools, wrap it in foil so that I don't have to handle it the day of the event, then freeze it. I heat up the bread at the site of the event.)

For events like Michael's birthday party, we used three coolers. When I catered, I had six big professional coolers, and I always requested a location with a kitchen, just in case we needed it.

People often ask me how to plan menus for such events. I think if you have a meat and a vegetable and something starchy (like potatoes or corn), a salad, and some kind of fruit, then you have a variety of all the food groups.

To me, cooking is serving. Sometimes I say I'm tired of serving, but that's not really so. Paul and I try to reach out to the young couples in our neighborhood. We've raised our children; we've overcome our problems; we've "been there and done that," so these young people are interested in our advice or someone who will just listen to them.

Often we take our hospitality on the road. We fill a basket with food and take it to someone who needs encouragement. Or we invite the neighbors over for dinner. We always have an open house at Christmas, and we encourage some of the neighborhood kids to come over to talk once in a while by having a supply of home-baked cookies on hand. (Also, I invite a few teenage girls over before Thanksgiving, and we make homemade pumpkin pies for their families.)

Cooking for others can be a part of your ministry too. There are always occasions to share with others to show you care. I love cooking for people who don't have time to cook, who don't like to cook, who are sick—or just because I want to give something away.

Michael and Debbie; Kimberly (our daughter) and David Bennett; me and Paul—Christmas 1996.

*C*HRISTMAS IS OUR FAVORITE TIME OF YEAR. **For almost as long as Paul and I have been married (forty-two years), we have opened our home to friends and neighbors.** The entire family also comes to our house on Christmas Eve.

On both occasions I like to prepare appetizers. Since this is a busy season, there are many items that you can prepare ahead and freeze.

I usually prepare Miniature Tacos (page 29), Shrimp and Sauce (page 12), Ham-Filled Rolls (page 19), Pineapple Cheese Ball and crackers (page 21), Sesame Chicken (page 20), Baked Spinach-Artichoke Spread (page 28), miniature Cream Puffs (page 191), and Raspberry Thumbprint Cookies (page 185). I serve fresh fruit with a variety of colors, like strawberries, honeydew melon, pineapple, and cantaloupe, accented with kiwifruit. The tacos, rolls (without ham), cream puffs (unfilled), and raspberry cookies can be prepared ahead of time and frozen.

We usually have fifty to sixty people for open house and twenty family members for Christmas Eve. If you're planning an open house, I recommend serving three to four salty items (meat, cheese, or vegetable), one fruit dish, three sweets, punch, and coffee. A variety of selections is good so that guests aren't tasting the same thing.

Kitchen Hint: When planning a party, check your recipes carefully. Choose some recipes that can be prepared ahead of time.

Crab Muffins

½ cup margarine (1 stick)
1 small can crabmeat
Dash of cayenne pepper
Paprika

1 jar (4 oz.) Old English cheese spread
4 green onions, chopped
5 English muffins

Cream the margarine and cheese. Add drained crabmeat, chopped onions, and cayenne. Split muffins into halves. Spread with crab mixture and cut each into 6 wedges. Freeze on a cookie sheet.

Store in plastic bags and use as needed. When ready to use, broil until slightly brown. Sprinkle with paprika and serve warm. *Yield:* 60 appetizers.

Grocery List: Old English cheese spread (in dairy section), 1 small can crabmeat, Green onions, 1 pkg. English muffins

Pantry Checklist: Margarine, Paprika, Cayenne pepper

Shrimp Sauce

1 bottle chili sauce
Juice of 2 lemons plus
    equal amount of sugar

½ jar (5 oz.) prepared horseradish
1 cup ketchup

Mix together and chill.

Grocery List: 1 bottle chili sauce, 1 5oz. jar horseradish, 2 lemons, Fresh parsley

Pantry Checklist: Sugar, Ketchup

Serve with a tray of shrimp garnished with parsley.

Kitchen Hint: After using part of the fresh parsley for garnish, chop and freeze the rest for future use.

Shrimp and Cheese Dip

1½ cups canned medium-size shrimp   2 Tbsp. lemon juice
1 cup ice water

Chill 30 minutes.

1 cup cream-style cottage cheese   5 Tbsp. chili sauce
1 tsp. onion, finely chopped   1 tsp. lemon juice
½ tsp. Worcestershire sauce   1 cup milk
2 Tbsp. sour cream   1 Tbsp. parsley, chopped
¼ tsp. salt   ⅛ tsp. white pepper

Drain shrimp and finely chop. Mix with remaining ingredients until smooth. Chill until ready to serve. Serve with party crackers. *Yield: 2 cups; 64 crackers.*

Grocery List: 1½ cups canned shrimp, 1 lb. cottage cheese, 1 bottle chili sauce, 8 oz. sour cream, Fresh parsley, Party crackers

Pantry Checklist: Lemon juice, Onion, Worcestershire sauce, Milk, Salt, White pepper

Shrimp Pizza

2 pkgs. (8 oz. each) soft cream cheese   3 jars shrimp cocktail
1 small onion, chopped   1 green pepper, chopped
1 can ripe olives, sliced   1 jar green olives
1 large pkg. shredded mozzarella cheese

Spread cream cheese on 10-inch plate. Next, spread shrimp evenly over cheese; add onion, pepper, and olives. Top with mozzarella cheese. Chill. Serve surrounded with crackers.

Grocery List: 2 (8 oz.) cream cheese, 3 jars shrimp cocktail, 1 green pepper, 1 can ripe olives, 1 jar green olives, 1 large pkg. mozzarella cheese

Pantry Checklist: Onion

Quick Spinach Dip

1 pkg. (10 oz.) frozen chopped spinach,
   thawed and drained
1 Tbsp. minced onion
1 Tbsp. mayonnaise

1 pkg. (0.4 oz.) ranch-style
   buttermilk dressing mix
1 carton (8 oz.) sour cream

Mix all ingredients. Chill, serve with vegetables or crackers.

Grocery List: 10 oz. frozen chopped spinach, 8 oz. sour cream,
1 pkg. ranch-style buttermilk dressing mix

Pantry Checklist: Mayonnaise, Onion

Bacon Squares

1 cup shredded Swiss cheese
1 green onion, chopped
8 slices bacon, cooked crisp and crumbled
Party rye bread

3 to 4 Tbsp. mayonnaise
½ tsp. celery salt

Mix all ingredients and spread on party rye bread. Bake at 350° for 10 minutes.

Grocery List: 1 pkg. shredded Swiss cheese, 1 lb. bacon, Green onions,
1 loaf party rye bread (in deli section)

Pantry Checklist: Mayonnaise, Celery salt

This recipe can be made ahead and frozen on a cookie sheet, ready to bake when
needed.

Surprise Pie

1 pkg. (8 oz.) cream cheese
2 Tbsp. minced onion
½ tsp. pepper
1 jar (2½ oz.) dried beef, cut with
scissors into small pieces

2 Tbsp. cream or milk
2 Tbsp. green pepper, chopped
½ cup sour cream
Chopped pecans

Combine ingredients, except pecans. Spread in shallow dish (pie plate) and top with chopped pecans. Bake at 350° for 15 minutes. Serve with crackers.

Grocery List: 8 oz. cream cheese, 1 green pepper, 1 jar (2½ oz.) dried beef,
8 oz. sour cream

Pantry Checklist: Cream or milk, Pepper, Onion, Pecans, Crackers

Vegetable Sandwich Filling

1 carrot, peeled
1 cucumber, sliced and cored
2 pkgs. (8 oz. each) cream cheese

1 green pepper, sliced
1 onion, peeled

Grate all vegetables with food processor. Blend with cream cheese and spread on party-shaped bread for tea sandwiches.

Grocery List: Carrots, Green pepper, 1 cucumber, 2 (8 oz.) cream cheese

Pantry Checklist: Onion

Kitchen Hint: To make party-shaped bread, use cookie cutters or a
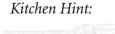   sharp knife. (Cut bread into triangles or whatever
shape is desired.)

Michael, 18 months old

Michael standing on
Uncle Frank's fire truck
in 1962

Michael, 5 years old

Musical Beginnings

When Michael was about five years old, we noticed he had begun to pick out tunes on the piano. He liked to "make up things"—melodies we had never heard before. In 1962 I had my wisdom teeth removed and had to stay home for a few weeks. Two ladies from our church, Kathleen Carpenter and Della Terry, always visited those who were sick. When they visited me and my family, we talked for a while. Then Mrs. Carpenter read some Scripture, and Mrs. Terry prayed.

As soon as she finished, Michael went over to the piano and began playing "Just As I Am." He thought he had been to church!

Meatballs with Sweet-and-Sour Sauce

2 lbs. ground beef
1 cup crushed cornflakes
1 tsp. salt
1 tsp. nutmeg
½ cup green pepper, chopped

2 eggs
1 cup bread crumbs
¼ tsp. pepper
1½ tsp. soy sauce
1 clove garlic, minced

Combine all ingredients; shape into bite-size meatballs. Bake at 400° about 15 minutes. Serve with Sweet-and-Sour Sauce. *Yield:* 80 meatballs.

Sweet-and-Sour Sauce

2 Tbsp. cornstarch
½ tsp. ground ginger
½ cup water
1 can (17 oz.) pineapple chunks, undrained

¼ cup cider vinegar
½ cup soy sauce
¼ cup brown sugar

Mix and heat all ingredients. Serve over meatballs in chafing dish.

Grocery List: 2 lbs. ground beef, 17 oz. can pineapple chunks, 1 small box cornflakes, 1 green pepper

Pantry Checklist: Salt, Pepper, Eggs, Nutmeg, Garlic, Bread crumbs, Soy sauce, Cornstarch, Brown sugar, Cider vinegar, Ginger

Sausage Balls

¼ cup ketchup
1 onion, chopped
3 cups cornflakes, crushed
Garlic powder to taste

2 lbs. lean ground beef
1 Tbsp. Worcestershire
  sauce
¾ to 1 cup milk

⅓ lb. sausage
2 eggs
¼ tsp. pepper
1 tsp. salt

Combine the ingredients; mix well. Roll into small balls and bake at 450° for 12 to 14 minutes. *Yield:* 30 servings.

Grocery List: 2 lbs. ground beef, 1 lb. sausage, 1 small box cornflakes,
                    Worcestershire sauce

Pantry Checklist: Ketchup, Onion, Eggs, Salt, Pepper, Garlic powder, Milk

Note: This recipe can be made ahead, baked, and frozen on cookie sheets. After the sausage balls freeze, place in plastic bags and reheat when ready to serve.

Asparagus Roll-ups

30 slices white or wheat bread,
  crusts removed
1 can asparagus spears, drained
¼ cup melted butter or margarine
¼ cup mayonnaise

1 pkg. (8 oz.) light cream cheese
Paprika
2 Tbsp. chives
¼ cup Parmesan cheese
½ tsp. Nature's Seasoning

Use a rolling pin to flatten each slice of bread. Combine cream cheese, chives, Nature's seasoning, and mayonnaise, mixing well. Spread cheese mixture on bread, covering to edges. Place 1 asparagus spear on each slice of bread; roll up and place seam side down on a greased baking sheet. Brush each with butter and sprinkle with Parmesan cheese and paprika. Bake at 400° for 12 minutes. *Yield:* 12 servings.

Grocery List: 2 loaves bread, 1 can asparagus spears, 8 oz. light
                    cream cheese, Chives, Parmesan cheese

Pantry Checklist: Mayonnaise, Nature's Seasoning, Butter, Paprika

Note: Prepare these ahead and freeze; bake just before serving.

Ham-Filled Rolls

1 pkg. dry yeast
1 tsp. sugar
½ cup warm water
½ cup shortening
1 egg, beaten
½ cup boiling water

⅓ cup sugar
1 tsp. salt
3 cups all-purpose flour
½ cup cold water
2 lbs. shaved ham

Cover yeast and 1 teaspoon sugar with ½ cup warm water; let sit for 5 minutes. Blend sugar and shortening; pour boiling water over and stir until melted. Add ½ cup cold water, yeast, beaten egg, salt, and flour. Refrigerate overnight or at least 2 hours.

Roll out dough, cut with small biscuit cutter, and let rise until doubled (about 1 hour). Bake at 375° about 10 minutes. Fill with sliced ham.

Grocery List: 1 small can shortening, 5 lbs. flour, 1 pkg. yeast, 2 lbs. shaved ham

Pantry Checklist: Sugar, Salt, Egg

Note: The above recipe can also be used for sweet rolls. Roll out dough and spread with butter, ½ cup sugar, and 2 teaspoons cinnamon, and roll up jelly-roll fashion. Cut into slices and put in roll pans, then let rise until doubled. Bake as above. Drizzle with your favorite icing.

Tea Sandwiches

1 loaf sandwich bread, crusts removed
1 can (8 oz.) crushed pineapple,
   drained well

Mayonnaise
1 pkg. (8 oz.) cream cheese
1 lb. shaved ham

Make a mixture of cream cheese and pineapple. Spread a slice of bread with this mixture; add another slice and spread with mayonnaise, then ham, and another slice of bread spread with mayonnaise. This makes a 3-layer sandwich. Cut into small tea sandwiches. These can be made and frozen ahead of time.

Grocery List: 1 loaf sandwich bread, 8 oz. can crushed pineapple, 8 oz. cream cheese, 1 lb. shaved ham

Pantry Checklist: Mayonnaise

Note: Reduced fat cream cheese may be used.

Sesame Chicken

24 chicken tenderloins
1 ½ cups buttermilk
2 Tbsp. lemon juice
1 tsp. soy sauce
1 tsp. paprika
1 Tbsp. Italian seasoning
1 tsp. salt

1 tsp. pepper
2 cloves garlic, minced
4 cups soft bread crumbs
¼ cup butter, melted
¼ cup shortening, melted
½ cup sesame seeds

Place chicken tenderloins in dish with a tight lid. Combine next 8 ingredients and pour over chicken. Cover and refrigerate overnight, occasionally turning bowl over to marinate well. When ready to bake, drain, roll in bread crumbs, drizzle with mixture of melted shortening and butter, and sprinkle with sesame seeds. Bake at 375° for 30 to 40 minutes or until well browned. Serve with sweet-and-sour sauce or cocktail sauce.

Grocery List: 24 chicken tenderloins, 1 qt. buttermilk, Italian seasoning, 2 garlic cloves, Sesame seeds (in spice section)

Pantry Checklist: Pepper, Salt, Butter, Paprika, Soy sauce, Lemon juice, Soft bread crumbs, Butter, Shortening

Creamy Beef and Cheese Ball

1 pkg. (8 oz.) cream cheese
1 jar (2½ oz.) dried beef, finely chopped
¼ tsp. Accent seasoning
2 Tbsp. green pepper, finely chopped
1 tsp. white pepper

¼ cup sour cream
2 Tbsp. milk
2 Tbsp. green onion, finely chopped
¼ cup chopped pecans

Mix together all ingredients, except nuts. Form ball or log and roll in nuts. Prepare 2 days ahead of serving time so flavors blend.

Grocery List: 8 oz. cream cheese, 2½-oz. jar dried beef, Pecans, 8 oz. sour cream, Green onions, 1 green pepper

Pantry Checklist: Accent seasoning, Milk, White pepper

Hot Cheese Balls

1 jar (5 oz.) Old English
    cheese spread

¼ cup butter
½ cup flour

Cream flour, butter, and cheese. Form into teaspoon-size balls. Chill 4 hours. Bake in preheated oven at 400° for 10 minutes. Balls will keep in refrigerator for 5 days. Good for parties.

Grocery List: 1 jar (5 oz.) Old English cheese spread (in dairy section)

Pantry Checklist: Butter, Flour

Pineapple Cheese Ball

2 pkgs. (8 oz. each) cream cheese
2 tsp. chopped onion
1 can (8½ oz.) crushed pineapple, drained
¼ cup green pepper, finely chopped
1 tsp. seasoned salt
2 cups pecans, finely chopped

Mix thoroughly; chill and shape in ball and roll in finely chopped pecans.

Grocery List: 2 pkgs. (8 oz.) cream cheese, pecans, 1 can (8½ oz.) crushed pineapple, 1 green pepper

Pantry Checklist: Onion, Seasoned salt

Kitchen Hint: Always garnish party foods with fresh flowers, parsley, or fresh fruit—whatever is appropriate with the food you're serving. Remember, presentation is important!

Festive Cream Cheese Ball

2 pkgs. (8 oz. each) cream cheese
2 Tbsp. chopped pimientos, drained
2 tsp. mustard

2 Tbsp. green onion, chopped
2 Tbsp. mayonnaise
Pecans, toasted and chopped

Mix first 5 ingredients together. Form into ball. Sprinkle with chopped, toasted pecans. *Note:* Better if made the day before.

*G*rocery List:
2 pkgs. (8 oz.) cream cheese, Green onions, 1 small jar pimientos, Pecans

*P*antry Checklist:
Mayonnaise, Mustard

Kitchen Hint:

To toast pecans, melt ¼ cup butter for every cup of pecans. Toss pecans in butter, then spread in shallow pan. Bake at 300° for 10 minutes.

Party Cheese Wreath

1 pkg. (8 oz.) shredded cheddar cheese
1 tsp. lemon juice
1 Tbsp. green onion, chopped
Chopped parsley (fresh) and
    red pepper for garnish

2 pkgs. (8 oz. each) cream cheese
1 Tbsp. red pepper, chopped
Dash cayenne pepper
1 tsp. Worcestershire sauce

Mix cheddar cheese and cream cheese together until well blended. Add lemon juice, red pepper, onion, cayenne pepper, and Worcestershire sauce; mix well. Refrigerate for several hours. Place a drinking glass in center of serving platter. Form cheese around glass to make a wreath. Remove glass; garnish with red pepper and chopped parsley.

*G*rocery List:
8 oz. shredded cheddar cheese, 1 red pepper, 2 pkgs. (8 oz. each) cream cheese, Green onion, Fresh parsley

*P*antry Checklist:
Lemon juice, Worcestershire sauce, Cayenne pepper

Cheese and Chili

2 cans (2.4 oz. each) chopped
   green chilies, drained
2½ cups shredded cheddar cheese

3 eggs, beaten
3 Tbsp. milk

Place chopped green chilies (drained) in bottom of greased 9-inch pie dish and top with cheese. Mix eggs and milk, pour on top, and bake at 325° for 45 minutes. Serve with crackers.

Grocery List: 2 (2.4 oz.) cans chopped green chilies, 1 lg. pkg. shredded cheddar cheese

Pantry Checklist: Milk, Eggs

Kitchen Hint: Reduce fat by using cooking spray whenever a recipe calls for a greased dish.

Chili and Pimiento Squares

4 cups shredded cheddar cheese
2 cans (2.4 oz. each) chopped green
   chilies, drained
1 tsp. minced onion

4 eggs, beaten
1 small jar diced
   pimientos, drained

Combine all ingredients in a medium bowl; stir well. Spread mixture in a lightly greased 8 x 8 baking dish and bake at 350° for 30 to 40 minutes. Let stand 10 minutes. Cut into squares and serve.

Grocery List: 2 lg. pkgs. shredded cheddar cheese, 2 cans chopped green chilies, 1 small jar diced pimientos

Pantry Checklist: Onion, Eggs

Chili con Queso

3 lbs. American cheese
2 onions, finely chopped
2 cans (20 oz. each) tomatoes, crushed
2 Tbsp. Worcestershire sauce

1 lb. cheddar cheese
8 cloves garlic, crushed
4 small cans chopped green chilies

Melt both kinds of cheese in double boiler; add other ingredients and cook until well blended (about 30 minutes). Serve hot in chafing dish with tortilla chips. Warm in double boiler before serving.

*G*rocery List:

> 3 lbs. American cheese, 1 lb. cheddar cheese, 2 onions,
> 8 cloves garlic, 2 (20 oz.) cans crushed tomatoes,
> 4 small cans green chilies

*P*antry Checklist:

> Worcestershire sauce

Note: If you don't have a double boiler, melt cheese in microwave or crockpot. Be careful not to scorch.

Layered Mexican Dip

1 pkg. (8 oz.) cream cheese, softened
1 jar (8 oz.) taco sauce or salsa (hot)
½ cup chopped green pepper
1 cup shredded mozzarella cheese

¼ cup mayonnaise
½ cup chopped green onion
1 cup chopped tomato
1 cup shredded cheddar cheese

Combine cream cheese and mayonnaise. Spread on a 9-inch plate. Top with taco sauce. Sprinkle onion, green pepper, and tomato over sauce. Top with shredded cheeses. Chill until serving time. Serve with tortilla chips.

*G*rocery List:

> 8 oz. cream cheese, 8-oz. jar taco sauce or salsa, Green onions,
> 1 green pepper, 1 tomato, 1 pkg. each mozzarella and
> cheddar cheeses (shredded)

*P*antry Checklist:

> Mayonnaise

The barn at Michael and Debbie's farm.

Special Holiday Events

Occasionally we hold big family events at Michael's farm, which has a big barn with lots of room. The downstairs is divided into two areas: one includes a family room and kitchen on the main level and bedrooms upstairs, and the other includes a stable with stalls for the horses and a small loft above, which would be a great place for kids to have a worship and praise time.

As an alternative to Halloween, Michael and Debbie hold a Harvest Party every October. They invite families to their farm and have a big bonfire to roast hot dogs. Everyone brings side dishes.

The first year they called their friends and told them about it. Apparently these people told others, because they ended up with seventy-five people. They had only forty hot dogs, so Michael went to the store twice to get more. (The closest grocery is several miles away.) They learned their lesson well—in 1998 they purchased so many hot dogs, they had eighty left.

One of the dishes I always bring for this event is Broccoli Delight Salad (page 90). Another dish that is a favorite is Homemade Salsa (page 26).

Homemade Salsa

2 Roma tomatoes, cut into quarters
¼ cup red pepper, cut into
   large pieces
½ cup onion, cut into large pieces
4 Tbsp. fresh cilantro, chopped
1 tsp. sugar

½ green pepper, cut into large pieces
1 can (4 oz.) green chilies,
   chopped and drained
1 can (14½ oz.) diced tomatoes
2 Tbsp. lime juice
Salt and pepper to taste

Chop pepper, onion, and chilies in food processor. Be careful not to blend until mushy. Add lime juice, cilantro, sugar, and salt and pepper. Blend quickly again. Add fresh tomatoes; blend quickly. Add canned tomatoes; again blend quickly.

Grocery List: 2 Roma tomatoes, 1 each green and red pepper, 4-oz. can green chilies, 1 can (14½ oz.) diced tomatoes, 1 bunch fresh cilantro, 1 lime

Pantry Checklist: Sugar, Salt, Pepper, Onion

Note: If you want a spicier salsa, add jalapeño or banana peppers.

Dill Dip

2 cups mayonnaise
1 Tbsp. seasoned salt
2 Tbsp. dill weed

2 cups sour cream
2 Tbsp. chopped parsley
2 Tbsp. dried onion flakes

Mix together and chill. Serve with raw vegetables.

Grocery List: 16 oz. sour cream, Dill weed, 1 jar mayonnaise

Pantry Checklist: Seasoned salt, Onion flakes, Parsley

Spinach Dip

1 pkg. (10 oz.) frozen chopped spinach, thawed and squeezed dry
1 carton (8 oz.) sour cream
1 cup mayonnaise (add more if needed)
1 can (8 oz.) sliced water chestnuts, chopped (may not need all)
1 small onion, chopped
1 pkg. Knorr or Lipton vegetable soup mix

Mix above ingredients and chill. Serve with vegetables, crackers, Hawaiian bread (cut out center, place dip inside, and cut the circle of bread you cut from the center into bite-size chunks), or hollowed purple cabbage.

 Grocery List: 10 oz. frozen chopped spinach, 8 oz. sour cream, 8-oz. can sliced water chestnuts, 1 pkg. vegetable soup mix, crackers (or Hawaiian bread or purple cabbage)

Pantry Checklist: Mayonnaise, Onion

Pepper Jelly

2 cups green or red pepper, ground   1 small fresh hot pepper
7½ cups sugar   1 ½ cups white vinegar
Few drops green food coloring if desired   1 bottle Sure Jell
   (or red, if red peppers are used)

Grind green or red pepper in food processor. Boil peppers, sugar, and vinegar 6 minutes. Add Sure Jell. Boil 3 minutes longer. Add food coloring. Pour in jars and seal. Serve over 8 oz. cream cheese with crackers.

Grocery List: 2 green or red peppers, 1 small hot pepper, 1 bottle Sure Jell, 1 bottle white vinegar, 8 oz. cream cheese, crackers

Pantry Checklist: Sugar, Green or red food coloring

Baked Spinach-Artichoke Spread

(Michael's favorite)

1 can (14 oz.) artichoke hearts, drained and chopped	⅛ tsp. garlic powder
1 pkg. (10 oz.) frozen chopped spinach, cooked and drained	Dash of cayenne pepper
	1 cup Parmesan cheese
	1 cup mayonnaise
1 cup shredded Monterey Jack or mozzarella cheese	Dash of Worcestershire sauce

Mix the above ingredients well, and spoon into a lightly greased 1-quart casserole or soufflé dish. Bake at 350° for 20 to 30 minutes. Serve with tortilla chips or crackers.

Grocery List: 1 (14 oz.) can artichoke hearts, 10-oz. pkg. frozen chopped spinach, 1 pkg. shredded Monterey Jack or mozzarella cheese, Worcestershire sauce, Cayenne pepper, Tortilla chips or crackers

Pantry Checklist: Mayonnaise, Parmesan cheese, Garlic powder

Ranch Sausage Cups

(another of Michael's favorites)

1 lb. cooked sausage, crumbled and drained well	1½ cups shredded sharp cheddar cheese
1½ cups shredded Monterey Jack cheese	1 cup prepared ranch salad dressing mix
½ cup chopped pimientos, drained	1 pkg. wonton wrappers

Combine first 5 ingredients and mix well. Spray muffin tins with cooking spray. Place wonton wrappers in muffin tins and bake at 350° 5 minutes or until golden brown. (They brown quickly.) Remove wrappers from oven; fill with sausage-cheese filling and bake 5 to 10 minutes more. *Note:* These are great served with a Mexican menu!

Grocery List: 1 lb. sausage, 1 pkg. each cheddar/Monterey Jack cheese, 1 pkg. ranch salad dressing mix, 1 small jar pimientos, 1 pkg. wonton wrappers

Pantry Checklist: Cooking spray

Appetizers

Hot Mexican Layered Dip

1 lb. ground chuck
1 can (15 oz.) black beans, drained
1 jar (16 oz.) salsa or picante sauce
Cheddar or Monterey Jack cheese

1 pkg. taco seasoning mix
1 can (10 oz.) Rotel tomatoes
Sour cream
Tortilla chips

Brown ground chuck and drain; add taco seasoning mix. Place black beans in bottom of small casserole dish sprayed with cooking spray; top with ground chuck mixture, Rotel tomatoes, and salsa. Top with cheese and bake at 350° for 30 minutes or until hot. Serve with sour cream and tortilla chips.

Grocery List: 1 can (15 oz.) black beans, 1 lb. ground chuck, 1 pkg. taco seasoning mix, 1 small jar (16 oz.) salsa or picante sauce, 1 can (10 oz.) Rotel tomatoes, Sour cream, 1 pkg. cheddar or Monterey Jack cheese, 1 pkg. tortilla chips

Miniature Tacos

1 lb. ground chuck
1 pkg. egg-roll wrappers
Cheddar cheese

1 pkg. taco seasoning mix
Sour cream

Brown ground chuck and drain well. Add taco seasoning mix according to directions. With scissors, cut egg-roll wrappers across twice, both ways. Cut a few slices at a time. This will make 9 stacks of small squares. Trim the corners from each of the stacks. Place egg-roll wrappers in miniature muffin tins and bake at 350° until brown, about 5 minutes. (These will brown very quickly, so watch them carefully.) Use the browned egg-roll wrappers for taco shells; they can be stored in a covered Tupperware dish. When ready to serve, place taco-beef mixture in chafing dish and serve with shells, sour cream, and grated cheese.

Grocery List: 1 lb. ground chuck, 1 pkg. taco seasoning mix, 1 pkg. egg-roll wrappers, Sour cream, 1 pkg. Shredded cheddar cheese

Kitchen Hint: The meat-taco mixture in the above recipe can be made ahead and frozen; also the browned egg-roll wrappers can be kept in freezer for several months.

Beverages

Kimberly Bennett, our daughter; me and Paul; and Michael at his farm.

*B*EVERAGES ARE AN IMPORTANT PART OF HOSPITALITY! Always offer your guests something hot or cold to drink.

On September 1, 1994, we moved to Franklin, Tennessee, from Kenova, West Virginia, to be close to Michael and our daughter, Kimberly. Kimberly was married October 1 of that year, so I had only one month to prepare for the wedding. Because we had many out-of-town guests, we hosted an open house at 10:00 A.M. the day of the wedding, in our 1,900-square-foot home, with over 100 people attending. I prepared Easy Garden Vegetable Pie squares (page 51), Ham-Filled Rolls (page 19), two kinds of Sweet Rolls (pages 57–58), Fresh Fruit (page 47), various breakfast breads—Spinach and Orange Bread (page 72), Carrot-Lemon Bread (page 69), and Banana Bread (page 71)— Bacon Squares (page 14), Fresh Orange Spritzer (page 36), and Hot Spiced Apple Cider (page 37).

Following our open house, everyone went to Kimberly and David's new home for punch and coffee, and the bride and groom opened all their gifts. I prepared Strawberry Punch (page 35) in advance and also served White Grape Spritzer (page 35). I always use a frozen ice ring (Kitchen Hint, page 38).

Prepare a punch that can be made and frozen ahead of time (add ginger ale at the last minute before serving). It's a great time-saver, and there are many good recipes. Also serve something hot—like tea or coffee. For a 30- to 50-cup coffeepot, measure one cup of coffee for every fifteen cups of water. For punch, plan 8 ounces per person (two punch cups).

That night Kimberly and David were married at Immanuel Baptist Church. The reception was held at a country club, and I didn't have to cook! The morning after the wedding, Kimberly and David stayed over and attended a brunch in their honor at Debbie and Michael's home with Debbie's mother and grandmother cohosting (another 100-plus people).

Banana Punch

4 cups sugar
5 bananas (very ripe)
1 can (6 oz.) frozen orange
  juice concentrate

6 cups water
1 can (12 oz.) frozen lemonade
1 can (46 oz.) pineapple juice
5 qts. ginger ale

Mix sugar and bananas in blender; add rest of ingredients, except for ginger ale. Place in quart containers and freeze. When ready to serve, let thaw about 20 minutes and pour 1 quart ginger ale over 1 quart of mix. *Yield:* 60 (4 oz.) servings.

Grocery List: 5 bananas, 12 oz. frozen lemonade, 6 oz. frozen orange juice, 46-oz. can pineapple juice, 3 2-liter bottles of ginger ale

Pantry Checklist: Sugar

Fran's Punch

4 bananas
1½ cups orange juice
3 cups water

1 can (46 oz.) pineapple juice
2 cups sugar
¼ cup lemon juice
Ginger ale

Mash bananas in food processor, then add rest of ingredients and blend. Pour mixture into ice cube trays and freeze. Serve cubes with ginger ale poured over them.

Note: You may substitute 18 packets of artificial sweetener for the sugar.

Grocery List: 46 oz. pineapple juice, 1 qt. orange juice, 4 bananas, 2 2-liter bottles of ginger ale

Pantry Checklist: Sugar or artificial sweetener, Lemon juice

Strawberry Punch

(served at Kim's open house for wedding)

2 cans (6 oz. each) frozen lemonade   1 cup sugar
1 pkg. (10 oz.) frozen strawberries   12 oz. water
                                  1 qt. ginger ale

Mix all ingredients except ginger ale in a blender and freeze. Thaw for about 30 minutes, and add 1 quart ginger ale when ready to serve. *Yield:* 20 (4 oz.) servings.

Grocery List: 12 oz. frozen lemonade, 10 oz. frozen strawberries, 1 qt. ginger ale

Pantry Checklist: Sugar

White Grape Spritzer

(Served at Kim's open house for wedding)

1 bottle (64 oz.) white grape juice, chilled
4 qts. ginger ale, chilled
1 pt. fresh strawberries, with caps

Mix white grape juice and ginger ale just before serving. Wash strawberries and float in punch bowl. *Yield:* 32 (4 oz.) servings.

Grocery List: 64 oz. white grape juice, 2 2-liter bottles ginger ale, 1 pt. fresh strawberries

Fresh Orange Spritzer

2 cans (6 oz. each) frozen orange juice
3 Tbsp. lemon juice

1 bottle (32 oz.) ginger ale
1 cup cold water

Mix all ingredients just before serving. Great for brunch! *Yield:* 13 (4 oz.) servings.

Grocery List: 1 can (12 oz.) frozen orange juice, 32 oz. ginger ale

Pantry Checklist: Lemon juice

Kitchen Hint: When figuring how much punch to make for a party, plan on 8 ounces (2 punch cups) per person.

Apricot Punch

1 can (46 oz.) apricot nectar
1 can (12 oz.) frozen orange juice
2 tsp. almond flavoring

1 can (46 oz.) pineapple juice
1 can (12 oz.) frozen lemonade
2 qts. ginger ale

Mix first 5 ingredients and freeze in food storage bags with zip closure. When ready to serve, thaw and mix with ginger ale.

Grocery List: 46 oz. apricot nectar, 46 oz. pineapple juice, 12 oz. each frozen orange juice and lemonade, 2 qts. ginger ale

Pantry Checklist: Almond flavoring

Spiced Tea

2 cups sugar
1 pkg. instant lemonade
2 tsp. ground cinnamon

2½ cups Tang powdered drink mix
½ cup instant tea (unsweetened)
1 tsp. cloves

Mix all ingredients and store in airtight container. Add 2 teaspoons per cup of hot water.

Grocery List: 1 large jar Tang, 1 pkg. instant lemonade, 1 small jar instant tea

Pantry Checklist: Sugar, Cinnamon, Cloves

Note: Spiced tea is a great gift idea. Be creative in how you package it! You can use decorative tins, jelly jars, and curling ribbon or raffia.

Hot Spiced Apple Cider

1 gallon apple cider or juice   4 cinnamon sticks

Combine cider and cinnamon sticks in a large pan. Bring to a boil, then simmer 30 minutes. *Yield:* 32 (4 oz.) servings.

Grocery List: 1 gal. apple cider

Pantry Checklist: Cinnamon sticks

Party Fruit Punch

2 cans (46 oz. each) pineapple juice
2 cans (12 oz. each) frozen orange juice (undiluted)
1 box (16 oz.) lemon gelatin (mixed with 1 cup boiling water)
4 qts. ginger ale

Mix together the first 3 ingredients; add 4 quarts ginger ale when ready to serve. Garnish with fruit slices. *Yield:* 64 (4 oz.) servings.

Grocery List:　　2 (46-oz.) cans pineapple juice, 24 oz. frozen orange juice, 16 oz. lemon gelatin, 4 qts. ginger ale (2 2-liter bottles)

Kitchen Hint:　　Make an ice ring to float in your punch—freeze fresh strawberries or red or green cherries in some of the punch. (Use a gelatin mold.)

Tea Punch

6 regular tea bags
1½ cups sugar
1 can (6 oz.) frozen orange juice
2 cups ginger ale or 7-Up

1 qt. boiling water
¼ cup Aspen mulling spices
1 can (6 oz.) frozen lemonade

Steep tea bags in boiling water for 10 minutes. Remove bags and add sugar and mulling spices; stir to dissolve. Add frozen juices, ginger ale or 7-Up, and enough water to make 1 gallon. Chill. *Yield:* 10 (4 oz.) servings.

Grocery List:　　6 oz. frozen orange juice, 6 oz. frozen lemonade, 1 qt. ginger ale, 1 pkg. Aspen mulling spices (sold in specialty stores)

Pantry Checklist:　　Tea bags, Sugar

Hot Wassail

3 cups pineapple juice
3 cups cranberry juice
1½ cups water
1 cup sugar

2 lemon slices
½ tsp. whole cloves
1 cinnamon stick

Heat together first 3 ingredients, then add sugar and heat until sugar is dissolved. Add remaining ingredients and let simmer at least 30 minutes. Serve hot. *Yield:* 20 (4 oz.) servings.

Grocery List: 24 oz. pineapple juice, 24 oz. cranberry juice, 1 lemon

Pantry Checklist: Sugar, Cinnamon sticks, Whole cloves

Sweetened Iced Tea

1 family-size tea bag
1½ cups boiling water
4½ cups cold water

2 small tea bags
¾ cup sugar

Steep tea bags in 1½ cups of boiling water for 5 minutes; add sugar and stir until dissolved. Add cold water. Serve. *Yield:* 6 (8 oz.) servings.

Grocery List: Family-size tea bags

Pantry Checklist: Sugar

Note: If you would like to cut down on sugar, add ¼ cup sugar, and artificial sweetener (4 to 5 packets) to taste.

Morning Occasions

Michael, Debbie, Kimberly, and David at Beano's Cabin (restaurant), overlooking Beaver Creek, Colorado.

*M*ORNING OCCASIONS ARE FUN TO PLAN. We enjoy the visits of our lifelong out-of-town friends, and I usually plan the breakfasts in advance. Easy Garden Vegetable Pie (page 51) is a favorite because it can be prepared, baked, and frozen in advance. Garlic Grits Casserole (page 57) can also be prepared one or two days before baking and serving. Sweet Rolls (page 58) can be prepared, baked, and frozen several weeks in advance.

Once a year, the entire family—Mike and Debbie; Kimberly and David; Debbie's parents, grandmother, and brother and his family; and Paul and I—spends a week in Colorado. We all share the planning of menus and grocery lists, then we divide the cooking responsibilities. I usually cook breakfast.

Debbie and Michael also take a trip each year to Colorado with their prayer group. They also share the cooking—even Michael! He cooks his famous French Toast (page 54). He even experimented with the recipe one morning for the kids and decided to dip it in cornflakes. They thought it was great! He calls it "Smitty's French Toast." He has always loved French toast and pancakes.

Shortly after he and Deb were married, she fixed French toast for him one morning. He started cutting into it and saw little green things.

"Debbie, what is this?" he asked.

Debbie, who is a health nut, had put alfalfa sprouts in his French toast! This is not a recipe Michael recommends.

He follows my standard recipe (page 54) and adds crushed cornflakes. He says the key to his recipe is the bread; his favorite is wheatberry bread. But the French toast must be topped by real maple syrup!

Debbie says real maple syrup is too expensive, so when Michael wants to use it, he buys it himself. This is so important to Michael that Debbie almost bought him a maple tree. In Maine or Vermont you can buy the rights to a tree, and they will send you all the maple syrup that comes from that tree. The cost seemed a little steep, or Debbie would have bought a tree!

Basic Crepe Batter

1 cup cold milk
4 eggs
½ tsp. salt

1 cup cold water
4½ Tbsp. melted cooled butter
1½ cups instant dissolving flour

Place milk, water, eggs, butter, and salt in blender first, then flour; whirl for 1 minute. Stop blender and, with a spatula, push down the flour on the sides and whirl again. You are ready to make crepes. This batter does not have to rest. *Yield:* 20 crepes.

Grocery List: 1 can instant dissolving flour

Pantry Checklist: Milk, Butter, Salt, Eggs

Nan's Pancakes

(Michael and Kim's grandmother; a favorite recipe)

1 egg
1¼ cups all-purpose flour
2 tsp. baking powder
½ tsp. salt

1¼ cups buttermilk
1 tsp. sugar
½ tsp. baking soda

Beat egg with buttermilk, then add rest of ingredients. Cook immediately on well greased griddle.

Grocery List: 1 qt. buttermilk

Pantry Checklist: Sugar, Baking powder, Baking Soda, Salt, Flour, Egg

Note: This is one of Michael's and his dad's favorite recipes. You can also add fresh blueberries to this recipe (my favorite!).

Kitchen Hint: Warm syrup or honey in the microwave before serving on pancakes.

Chicken Supreme Crepe

4 chicken breasts
2 Tbsp. melted butter
2 cups Sherry Wine
   Sauce (recipe follows)
3 Tbsp. cooking wine
¼ tsp. tarragon

1 cup sliced mushrooms
2 hard-boiled eggs, diced finely
1 cup shredded mozzarella cheese
3 Tbsp. chopped parsley
Salt and pepper to taste
1 cup shredded Parmesan cheese

Cook chicken breasts; cool and chop. Make crepes according to the Basic Crepe Batter recipe (page 44). Sauté mushrooms in butter; add 1 cup sherry wine sauce, chicken, hard-boiled eggs, 1½ tablespoons parsley, 3 tablespoons cooking wine, and salt and pepper to taste. Add tarragon last and simmer 2 minutes. Spoon into crepes; fold seam side down. Place in buttered baking dish. Cover with remaining sauce and sprinkle with Parmesan and mozzarella cheese. Heat at 375° for 15 to 20 minutes. *Yield:* 16 crepes.

Sherry Wine Sauce

2 Tbsp. butter
2 cups milk
1 egg yolk
Pinch of nutmeg

2 Tbsp. flour
Salt and pepper to taste
1 tsp. cooking sherry

Melt butter; add flour and stir with a whisk. Let foam and cook for 1 minute. Slowly add milk, stirring constantly, until thickened. Add rest of ingredients.

Grocery List: 4 chicken breasts, 1 box tarragon (in spice section), 1 can sliced mushrooms, 1 bottle cooking wine, Fresh parsley, 1 small pkg. shredded mozzarella cheese, Parmesan cheese

Pantry Checklist: Eggs, Butter, Flour, Milk, Salt, Pepper, Nutmeg

Serving suggestion: Fresh steamed broccoli (with lemon butter sauce) and Minced Peach Halves (page 49).

Michael works in the basement studio of his home in 1989.

Dove Award Brunches

We have been going to the Dove Awards for years. Some years we have had from fifteen to twenty friends and family come from West Virginia because they love Michael and have watched him grow up. The day after the awards I sometimes host a brunch at Michael's for our guests and family; this has always been a special time for everyone to visit.

In 1999 Michael received six Dove Awards (among them, Artist of the Year, the top award). He was also given the prestigious Golden Note Award, a lifetime achievement award from ASCAP.

The Dove Award Brunch menu usually includes: Sausage Breakfast Casserole (page 50), Ham-Filled Rolls (page 19), Garlic Grits Casserole (page 57), Crunchy Potato Bites (page 55), Cinnamon Rolls (page 61), Orange Sweet Rolls (page 57), Fresh Fruit (page 47), and Fresh Orange Spritzer (page 36).

Whipped Cream Fruit Dressing

1 egg, beaten
2 Tbsp. pineapple juice
3 Tbsp. sugar

2 Tbsp. lemon juice
½ cup whipped cream
or whipped topping

Combine first 4 ingredients and cook until thick, stirring constantly; cool. Add ½ cup whipped cream or whipped topping. Chill. Serve with fresh fruit.

Grocery List: 1 small can pineapple juice, 1 pt. whipping cream or 1 small (8 oz.) whipped topping

Pantry Checklist: Sugar, Lemon juice, Egg

Orange Fruit Dressing

1 cup whipped topping
¼ cup Tang powdered drink mix

¼ cup mayonnaise

Mix the above ingredients together and serve as a dip for fresh fruit.

Grocery List: 8 oz. whipped topping, 1 jar Tang

Pantry Checklist: Mayonnaise

Fresh Fruit

Always choose fruit according to color and taste. My favorite combination is cantaloupe, honeydew melon, pineapple, strawberries, and blueberries or purple grapes. Garnish top with kiwifruit. The night before serving, cut cantaloupe, pineapple, and honeydew melon into chunks. Package separately in plastic bags; check for sweetness; if not sweet enough, add a couple of packets of artificial sweetener to enhance flavor; store in refrigerator overnight. The next morning you can mix and add additional fruit. For fruit that discolors easily, dip in lemon juice or clear carbonated soda.

Hot Spiced Fruit

1 pkg. (12 oz.) dried pitted prunes
1 can (29 oz.) peach halves,
    drained (reserve juice)
1 can cherry pie filling
½ cup brown sugar

1 pkg. (6 oz.) dried apricots
1 can (20 oz.) pineapple chunks,
    drained (reserve juice)
½ cup butter, melted

Spray 9 x 13 baking dish with cooking spray; place fruit in dish. Melt butter; add sugar and juices. Pour over fruit and bake at 350° for 1 hour.

Grocery List: 1 pkg. (12 oz.) dried pitted prunes, 1 pkg. (6 oz.) dried apricots, 29 oz. can peach halves, 1 can cherry pie filling

Pantry Checklist: Butter, Brown sugar

Pineapple Soufflé

1½ sticks butter
3 eggs
1 can (16 oz.) crushed pineapple
    (drain half of the juice)

1¼ cups sugar
4 to 6 slices bread, cubed with
    crusts removed

Cream butter, sugar, and eggs (1 at a time). Add pineapple and stir in bread. Place in ungreased 9 x 13 dish and bake at 350° for 1 hour (covered). Uncover and broil for 5 minutes or until brown on top.

Grocery List: 1 loaf white bread, 1 can (16 oz.) crushed pineapple

Pantry Checklist: Butter, Sugar, Eggs

Minced Peach Halves

2 cans (29 oz.) peach halves   1 jar mincemeat

Place mincemeat in center of peach halves and bake at 350° just until warm (about 10-12 minutes). Great served with brunch!

Grocery List: 1 can peach halves, 1 jar mincemeat

Quiche

Pie crust in quiche dish   4 slices cooked bacon, crumbled
1 green onion, chopped   ¾ cup shredded cheddar cheese
¾ cup shredded Swiss cheese   4 eggs, beaten
2 cups milk   ¼ tsp. salt
¼ tsp. white pepper   Dash of nutmeg
1 Tbsp. flour

Bake pie crust at 400° for 4 minutes. Place bacon, onion, and cheeses in crust. Combine remaining ingredients and pour over top. Bake at 350° for 1 hour.

Grocery List: 1 dozen eggs, 1 qt. milk, 1 pkg. each shredded Swiss and cheddar cheese, Green onion, 1 lb. bacon

Pantry Checklist: Flour, Salt, White pepper, Nutmeg

Note: You can substitute 1 cup of the following for bacon: broccoli, spinach, or mushrooms. You can use ½ cup of cubed ham, fresh broccoli, carrots, cauliflower, or green peppers in the above quiche also.

Kitchen Hint: Remember, it is healthier to grate your own cheese; there is an additive in grated cheese to prevent the cheese from sticking together.

Sausage Breakfast Casserole

6 slices bread
1½ cups (6 oz.) shredded
  cheddar cheese
1 tsp. salt

1 lb. sausage
6 eggs, beaten
2 cups milk

Remove crusts from bread, place bread in a greased 13 x 9 x 2 baking dish, and set aside. Cook sausage until browned, stirring to crumble; drain well. Spoon over bread slices; sprinkle with cheese. Combine eggs, milk, and salt; mix well and pour over cheese. Cover casserole and chill overnight.

Remove from refrigerator 15 minutes before baking. Bake uncovered at 350° for 45 minutes or until set. *Yield:* 8 servings.

Grocery List: 1 loaf white bread, 1 lb. sausage, 1 small pkg. shredded cheddar cheese, 1 dozen eggs, 1 qt. milk

Pantry Checklist: Salt

Note: If you are pressed for time or are planning ahead, you can prepare this dish with the bread, sausage, and cheese and then freeze. The night before serving, add rest of ingredients, place in refrigerator, and bake the next morning.

Cheese Soufflé

4 Tbsp. butter
1½ cups milk
Dash of cayenne pepper
½ lb. sharp cheddar cheese

4 Tbsp. flour
1 tsp. salt
6 eggs, separated

Melt butter; add flour and blend. Add milk and cook until thickened, stirring constantly. Add salt, cayenne, and cheese. Heat until cheese is melted. Add beaten egg yolks. Cook about 5 minutes, then pour into very stiffly beaten egg whites. Mix well. Bake in 2-quart baking dish at 300° for 50 minutes.

Grocery List: 1 qt. milk, 1 small pkg. shredded cheddar cheese, 1 dozen eggs

Pantry Checklist: Butter, Flour, Salt, Cayenne pepper

Easy Garden Vegetable Pie

2 cups chopped fresh broccoli, cooked,
   or 1 pkg. frozen chopped broccoli,
   cooked and drained
1 cup shredded cheese
   (cheddar or Swiss)
1 tsp. salt
1 Tbsp. Worcestershire sauce

½ cup chopped onion
½ cup chopped green pepper
1½ cups milk
¾ cup Bisquick baking mix
3 eggs
½ tsp. cayenne pepper

Heat oven to 400°. Lightly grease a 9 x 13 baking dish. Mix broccoli (or spinach), onion, green pepper, and cheese in pie plate. Beat remaining ingredients until smooth. Pour over other ingredients; bake until golden brown and knife inserted comes out clean, 35 to 40 minutes.

Grocery List: 10 oz. pkg. frozen chopped broccoli or fresh broccoli, 1 green pepper, 1 small pkg. shredded cheese, 1 qt. milk, 1 box Bisquick baking mix

Pantry Checklist: Salt, Onion, Cayenne pepper, Worcestershire sauce, Eggs

Note: Frozen spinach (10 oz. chopped) may be used in this recipe. You can reduce the fat by using reduced-fat biscuit baking mix. This can be made ahead of time, baked, and frozen. Heat thoroughly before serving. It makes a great appetizer; just cut into small squares!

Breakfast Casserole

6 slices bread, crust removed
Butter
1 tsp. salt
4 eggs

2 cups shredded cheddar cheese
1 tsp. dry mustard
1 Tbsp. Worcestershire sauce
2½ cups milk

Grease bottom and sides of casserole dish. Line bottom with bread; cover with cheese and dot with butter. Beat remaining ingredients together and pour over cheese. Refrigerate overnight. Bake at 350° for 30 minutes.

Grocery List: 1 loaf white bread, 1 pkg. shredded cheddar cheese, 1 dozen eggs, 1 qt. milk

Pantry Checklist: Dry mustard, Salt, Butter, Worcestershire sauce

Reuben Brunch Casserole

10 slices rye bread,
   cut into ¾-inch cubes
2½ cups (10 oz.) shredded Swiss cheese
¼ tsp. pepper

1½ lbs. cooked corned beef
6 eggs, lightly beaten
3 cups milk

Spray 13 x 9 x 2 glass baking dish with cooking spray; arrange bread cubes in bottom of dish. Coarsely shred corned beef with knife. Layer meat over bread. Sprinkle with cheese. Beat eggs, milk, and pepper in bowl until well blended. Pour over corned beef mixture. Cover with foil. Refrigerate overnight. Bake covered at 350° for 45 minutes, then uncovered for 10 minutes, or until bubbly and puffed. Serve immediately.

Grocery List: 1 loaf rye bread, 1½ lbs. corned beef, 1 dozen eggs, 1 qt. milk, 1 large pkg. shredded Swiss cheese

Pantry Checklist: Pepper

Ham and Cheese Casserole

16 slices bread, trimmed and cubed
1 lb. ham, cubed or minced in processor
½ cup shredded Swiss cheese
½ tsp. onion salt
3 cups cornflakes, crushed

2 cups shredded cheddar cheese
6 eggs
3 cups milk
½ tsp. dry mustard
½ cup margarine, melted

Grease a large baking dish. Spread half of bread cubes in dish; add ham and cheeses. Cover with remaining bread cubes. Mix eggs, milk, onion salt, and dry mustard. Pour over bread mixture and refrigerate overnight. Next morning combine cornflakes and melted margarine and sprinkle over casserole. Bake at 375° for 40 minutes. Let stand 10 minutes before serving.

Grocery List: 1 loaf bread, 1 lb. ham, 1 qt. milk, 1 dozen eggs, 1 lg. pkg. shredded cheddar cheese, 1 small pkg. shredded Swiss cheese, 1 box cornflakes

Pantry Checklist: Dry mustard, Onion salt, Margarine

Michael poses in 1967 with his favorite Christmas presents—
his guitar, football, and basketball.

The Young Musician

Michael's grandmother, Mary Smith, was an organist and pianist for forty years. She began to teach Michael piano lessons when he was about five years old. Even at that age, she saw something unusual about his musical ability.

He would say, "Nanny, if you would just play it once for me, I think I can get it." He had that gift from God, a perfect ear.

She continued giving him lessons until he was about fifteen or sixteen. She was a very special member of our family, and her recipes are throughout this book. (Look for Nan's recipes.)

Michael's dad has a wonderful voice (although he would never admit it), so there are some great musical genes in Michael's background. Michael and his sister, Kimberly, both accompanied choirs in our church. (Michael accompanied the youth choir and Kimberly played for the sanctuary choir.)

Mom's French Toast

3 eggs, lightly beaten   ⅓ cup milk
¼ tsp. salt   ¼ tsp. cinnamon
1 tsp. vanilla   8 slices bread

Mix first 5 ingredients. Dip bread in egg mixture and sauté in butter, turning once and adding more butter as necessary until browned and crisp. Sprinkle with powdered sugar and serve with maple syrup.

Grocery List: 1 loaf bread, Maple syrup

Pantry Checklist: Eggs, Milk, Salt, Vanilla, Cinnamon, Powdered sugar

Smitty's French Toast

3 eggs, lightly beaten   ¼ tsp. cinnamon
¼ tsp. salt   8 slices wheatberry bread
1 tsp. vanilla   Cornflakes (optional)
⅓ cup milk

Mix first 5 ingredients. Dip bread in egg mixture and sauté in butter, turning once and adding more butter as necessary until browned and crisp. Sprinkle with powdered sugar. Michael likes *pure* maple syrup!

Grocery List: 1 loaf wheatberry bread, Maple syrup

Pantry Checklist: Milk, Salt, Vanilla, Cinnamon, Eggs, Powdered sugar

Note: After dipping bread in egg mixture, roll in crushed cornflakes for a different, crunchy taste!

Night Before French Toast

1 loaf French or Italian bread,
   sliced thick
4 tsp. sugar
½ tsp. cinnamon
2 Tbsp. butter, cut into small pieces

8 large eggs
3 cups milk
¾ tsp. salt
1 Tbsp. vanilla

Use extra butter to grease a 9 x 13 baking dish. Arrange bread in one layer in bottom of dish. In large bowl, whisk eggs with remaining ingredients, except butter. When thoroughly mixed, pour over bread. Cover with foil and refrigerate overnight. To bake, uncover and dot with 2 tablespoons butter and bake at 350° for 45 to 50 minutes until bread is puffy and lightly browned. Remove from oven and let stand 5 minutes before serving.

Grocery List: 1 loaf French or Italian bread

Pantry Checklist: Sugar, Salt, Cinnamon, Vanilla, Butter, Eggs, Milk

Crunchy Potato Bites

1 cup cooked mashed potatoes
½ cup shredded Swiss cheese
1 egg, beaten
1 tsp. prepared mustard
Dash of pepper
1 cup crushed cornflakes

1 cup cooked ham, ground
2 Tbsp. green onion, chopped
3 Tbsp. mayonnaise
¼ tsp. cayenne pepper
Salt to taste

Cook sliced potatoes in salted water until done, about 20 minutes. Drain, add butter or margarine, and blend with mixer until creamy. Combine all ingredients except cornflakes. Shape mixture into 1-inch balls; roll in crushed cornflakes. Place on lightly greased baking sheets; bake at 350° for 30 minutes.

Grocery List: 2 to 3 potatoes, 1 small pkg. ham, 1 small pkg. Swiss cheese, 1 small box cornflakes, Green onions

Pantry Checklist: Eggs, Mustard, Cayenne pepper, Mayonnaise, Pepper, Salt

Note: Leftover mashed potatoes can be used for this recipe.

Mexican Brunch Pie

5 eggs, beaten
2 Tbsp. margarine or butter, melted
½ tsp. baking powder
¼ cup flour
½ tsp. salt

1 carton (8 oz.) small-curd
cottage cheese
2 cups Monterey Jack cheese
1 can (4 oz.) chopped green
chilies, drained

Combine first 5 ingredients in a large bowl; beat well at medium speed. Stir in remaining ingredients and pour into a well-greased 9-inch pie plate. Bake at 400° for 10 minutes; reduce heat to 350° and bake about 20 minutes or until done.

Grocery List: 1 dozen eggs, 1 8-oz. carton cottage cheese, 1 lg. pkg. shredded Monterey Jack cheese, 1 4-oz. can green chilies

Pantry Checklist: Margarine, Flour, Baking powder, Salt

Miniature Sausage Muffins

½ lb. sausage
¾ cup biscuit mix
¼ tsp. cayenne pepper
½ cup shredded cheddar cheese

⅓ cup chopped green onion
½ tsp. dry mustard
½ cup milk

Cook sausage and green onions over medium heat until sausage is browned, stirring to crumble. Drain well. Combine remaining ingredients and stir just until moistened. Stir in sausage mixture and spoon into greased miniature muffin pans. Bake at 400° for 12 to 14 minutes.

Grocery List: 1 lb. sausage, Green onions, 1 small box biscuit mix, 1 small pkg. shredded cheddar cheese

Pantry Checklist: Dry mustard, Cayenne pepper, Milk

Garlic Grits Casserole

½ cup quick-cooking grits, uncooked   1 roll (6 oz.) garlic cheese, cubed
¼ cup melted margarine   2 eggs, slightly beaten
1 cup milk

Cook grits according to package directions. Add cheese and margarine, stirring until cheese melts. Combine eggs and milk; stir into grits. Spoon into a lightly greased 1-quart casserole. Bake at 350° for 45 minutes, or until golden brown and set. *Yield:* 4 servings.

*G*rocery List: 1 box quick-cooking grits, 6 oz. roll of garlic cheese (in dairy section)

*P*antry Checklist: Margarine, Eggs, Milk

Note: This casserole can be mixed the night before, put in refrigerator, and baked the next morning.

Orange Sweet Rolls

1 pkg. dry yeast   ½ cup cold water   soft margarine
1 tsp. sugar   1 egg, beaten   2 cups powdered sugar
½ cup warm water   1 tsp. salt   ½ cup orange juice
⅓ cup sugar   3 cups all-purpose flour
½ cup shortening   2 Tbsp. orange peel, grated
½ cup boiling water   ½ cup sugar

Cover yeast and 1 teaspoon sugar with ½ cup warm water. Blend ⅓ cup sugar with shortening; pour boiling water over and stir until melted. Add ½ cup cold water, yeast mixture, egg, salt, and flour. Refrigerate overnight or at least 2 hours.

    Roll out dough and spread with soft margarine, grated orange peel, and ½ cup sugar. Roll up jelly-roll style and slice. Place in muffin pans; let rise for at least 1 hour. Bake at 350° for about 15 minutes, or until brown. Make glaze of powdered sugar and orange juice; spread over warm rolls.

*G*rocery List: 1 pkg. dry yeast, 5 lbs. flour, 1 orange, Tub of margarine

*P*antry Checklist: Eggs, Salt, Sugar, Shortening, Powdered sugar

Sour Cream Coffee Cake

½ cup chopped pecans
2 Tbsp. brown sugar
2 cups sugar
1 cup sour cream
2 cups all-purpose flour
¼ tsp. salt

1 Tbsp. cinnamon
2 sticks margarine
2 eggs
1 tsp. vanilla
1 tsp. baking powder

Combine nuts, cinnamon, and brown sugar and set aside. Cream margarine and sugar; add eggs and beat thoroughly. Add sour cream and vanilla; mix well. Add flour, baking powder, and salt. Pour half of mixture into a greased and floured springform pan. Sprinkle with half of cinnamon mixture. Pour in rest of batter. Add remaining topping. Bake at 350° for 50 to 60 minutes, or until done. Cool; sprinkle with powdered sugar.

Grocery List: 1 pkg. pecans, 1 lb. margarine, 1 pt. sour cream

Pantry Checklist: Brown sugar, Cinnamon, Vanilla, Sugar, Baking powder, Salt, Flour, Eggs, Powdered sugar

Sweet Rolls

¼ cup oil
1½ cups hot water
Butter
1 pkg. dry yeast (quick-rise)

¼ cup sugar
3 to 3½ cups all-
    purpose flour
Cinnamon

1 tsp. salt
Icing:
2 cups powdered sugar
½ cup water

Using a large mixer with dough hook, mix oil, sugar, salt, and hot water. Add 1 cup flour and yeast; beat well. Add remaining flour. Mix well and place in well-greased bowl. Cover and let rise until doubled.

Punch down and roll out on lightly floured board. Spread butter on one side of dough; sprinkle with cinnamon. (Add 1 cup pecans if you like.) Roll up jelly-roll fashion and slice. Place slices in well-greased cake pans. Let rise until doubled. Bake at 350° for 15 minutes or until brown. Ice cool rolls with glaze of powdered sugar and water.

Grocery List: 1 pkg. quick-rise yeast, 1 pkg. pecans (optional)

Pantry Checklist: Flour, Oil, Salt, Sugar, Powdered sugar, Cinnamon, Butter

Easy Orange Breakfast Ring

1 cup sugar
4 cans refrigerated flaky biscuits
Grated rind from 1 orange

1 cup powdered sugar
2-3 Tbsp. orange juice

Mix sugar and orange rind; cut each biscuit into 4 pieces and coat with sugar mixture. Overlap biscuits in greased bundt pan and bake at 350° for 30 to 40 minutes. Let cool for 10 minutes, then turn out onto plate. Mix powdered sugar and orange juice to make glaze, and pour over top.

Grocery List: 4 cans refrigerated flaky biscuits, 1 orange, Orange juice

Pantry Checklist: Sugar, Powdered sugar

Caramel Sweet Rolls

½ cup sugar
1 Tbsp. salt
3 cups hot water
½ cup oil
5 to 6 cups all-purpose flour
2 pkgs. quick-rise yeast

Brown Sugar Mixture:
2 cups brown sugar
1½ cups chopped pecans
1 cup margarine, melted
1 cup light corn syrup

Using a large mixer with dough hook, mix first 4 ingredients and 2 cups flour. Add yeast and 1 cup flour. Continue adding flour gradually until dough no longer has a shine. Place dough in large greased bowl and turn over so all sides are greased; cover with tea towel and let rise until doubled. Punch down and make rolls by shaping into small balls.

    Combine melted margarine, brown sugar, corn syrup, and pecans. Pour evenly among 3 greased round cake pans. Place rolls in pans. Let rise until doubled; bake at 350° for 16 to 18 minutes or until browned. Invert rolls onto serving plate and let stand, covered with pan, 2 minutes. Remove pan, scraping any remaining pecan mixture from pan onto rolls.

Grocery List: 5 lb. flour, 2 pkgs. quick-rise yeast, 1 bottle light corn syrup, 1 box brown sugar, 1 pkg. chopped pecans

Pantry Checklist: Sugar, Salt, Oil, Margarine

Michael—12 years old.

Michael—17 years old.

Graduation from Credo-Kenova
High School in 1976.

Michael returns home for a visit after he moved to Nashville.

Family Album Pictures

Here are some of the pictures we showed at Michael's 40th birthday party. People often kid Michael about his various hair styles throughout the years. Here are a few examples.

Cinnamon Rolls

(Michael's favorite)

½ cup warm water	1 tsp. salt	½ stick butter
1 tsp. sugar	½ cup boiling water	¼ cup cinnamon
1 pkg. dry yeast	½ cup cold water	½ cup sugar
½ cup shortening	1 egg, beaten	*Icing:*
⅓ cup sugar	3 cups all-purpose flour	2 cups powdered sugar
		½ cup water

Mix warm water, 1 teaspoon sugar, and yeast; let rise. Mix shortening, ⅓ cup sugar, and salt. Pour boiling water over mixture; stir until melted. Add ½ cup cold water, egg, yeast mixture, and flour. Place in refrigerator overnight. Roll out thinly and spread with butter, cinnamon, and sugar. Roll up jelly-roll fashion, slice, and place in 2 round cake pans. Let rise till double in size. Bake at 350° for about 15 minutes. Ice cool rolls with glaze of powdered sugar and water.

Grocery List: 1 pkg. dry yeast, 5 lbs. flour

Pantry Checklist: Shortening, Sugar, Salt, Cinnamon, Egg, Powdered sugar, Butter

Note: These sweet rolls can be made ahead and frozen. When ready to use, heat rolls and add icing.

Cinnamon Roll-ups

Cinnamon and sugar	24 slices fresh white bread,
½ cup butter	crusts trimmed
1 pkg. (8 oz.) cream cheese	¼ cup butter, melted
½ cup sugar	

Mix cinnamon and sugar. Cream together butter, cream cheese, and sugar. Roll bread slices with rolling pin and spread with cream cheese mixture. Roll up, brush with melted butter, and roll in cinnamon and sugar mixture. Bake at 375° for 15 minutes.

Grocery List: 1 loaf white bread, 8 oz. cream cheese

Pantry Checklist: Sugar, Butter, Cinnamon

Graham Cracker Brunch Cake

Graham Cracker Mixture:

2 cups graham cracker crumbs
¾ cup brown sugar
¾ cup margarine or butter, melted

¾ cup chopped pecans
1¼ tsp. cinnamon

Mix together and set aside.

1 pkg. yellow cake mix
¼ cup oil

1 cup water
3 eggs

Mix together and place in greased 9 x 13 pan. Pour half of graham cracker mixture on batter and swirl through batter with a fork. Top with remaining mixture and bake at 350° for 45 minutes. Ice with following:

Icing:

2 cups powdered sugar   4 Tbsp. milk   1 tsp. vanilla

Grocery List: 1 yellow cake mix, 1 box graham cracker crumbs, 1 pkg. chopped pecans, 1 box powdered sugar

Pantry Checklist: Oil, Eggs, Vanilla, Milk, Margarine, Cinnamon, Brown Sugar

Cinnamon Pecan Coffee Cake

1 box yellow cake mix
4 eggs

1 cup sour cream   ¾ cup oil
½ cup sugar

Mix all of the above and place in a 9 x 13 pan or bundt pan. Swirl the following mixture into cake mix.

1 cup brown sugar   1 cup pecans   4 tsp. cinnamon

Bake at 350° for 45 to 50 minutes.

Icing:

2 cups powdered sugar   4 to 5 Tbsp. milk   1 tsp. vanilla

Mix together and pour over warm cake.

Grocery List: 1 yellow cake mix, 1 doz. eggs, 1 pt. sour cream, 1 box powdered sugar, 1 pkg. chopped pecans

Pantry Checklist: Oil, Sugar, Brown sugar, Cinnamon, Milk, Vanilla

Bran Muffins

1 cup oil
2 tsp. salt
5 tsp. baking soda
1 box (20 oz.) raisin
  bran cereal

4 eggs
3 cups sugar
3 cups white flour
1 qt. buttermilk

1 Tbsp. pumpkin pie spice
2 cups wheat flour
2 cups chopped pecans or
  walnuts

Mix oil, eggs, and buttermilk; then add dry ingredients, cereal, and pecans. (This may be kept in refrigerator 8 days.) When ready to bake, place in greased muffin tins and sprinkle with cinnamon sugar. Bake at 400° for 23 minutes.

Grocery List: 1 dozen eggs, 1 qt. buttermilk, 1 small bag wheat flour, 1 box (20 oz.) raisin bran cereal, 1 pkg. pecans

Pantry Checklist: Oil, Salt, Sugar, Pumpkin pie spice, White flour, Baking soda

Blueberry Muffins

1½ cups all-purpose flour
½ cup sugar
2 tsp. baking powder
½ tsp. salt
1 egg, lightly beaten

½ cup milk
¼ cup sour cream
¼ cup vegetable oil
1 pt. fresh blueberries

Combine first 4 ingredients in a large bowl; make a well in center of mixture. Combine egg, milk, sour cream, and oil; add liquid mixture to dry ingredients, stirring just until moistened. Stir in blueberries. Spoon into greased muffin pans, filling two-thirds full. Bake at 400° for 20 minutes or until brown. Remove muffins from pans immediately.

Grocery List: 1 pt. fresh blueberries, 1 pt. sour cream

Pantry Checklist: Sugar, Flour, Baking powder, Salt, Milk, Oil, Egg

Kitchen Hint: Muffins will slide right out of pan if it is placed on a wet towel.

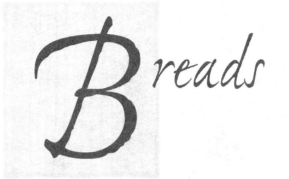

Breads

Michael and Debbie in Colorado.

*B*READ IS PROBABLY ONE OF MY FAVORITE THINGS TO PREPARE, and I couldn't even guess how many loaves I have baked over the years. I have a large Kitchen Aid mixer and can make three loaves with one recipe.

This past Christmas our entire family gathered at Debbie and Michael's home on Christmas night. (There were forty-seven of us!) I baked sixteen loaves of bread ahead of time and froze them. When our family has a potluck dinner, Debbie and Michael always ask me to bring bread and Whipped Butter (page 68).

There are many different things you can do with one basic recipe: Cinnamon Rolls (page 61), Caramel Sweet Rolls (page 59), and Cloverleaf Rolls (page 74).

Debbie and I volunteered to teach two Horizon cooking classes for seventh graders at Christ Presbyterian Academy where their children attend school. For the first session, I taught bread-making to the seven girls in the class and showed them the many things they could do with one recipe; we made cinnamon rolls, loaf bread, ham biscuits, and dinner rolls. I let them mix the dough, roll it out, and then bake it.

During the second session, Debbie and I showed them how to prepare and creatively package the breads, sweet rolls, and biscuits for gifts. The seventh graders colored the icing and drizzled it over the sweet rolls to make them attractive and then creatively packaged their gifts.

Homemade breads make wonderful gifts. You can package fruit breads in colored plastic wrap and tie raffia or colorful curling ribbon around them. Or make plain loaf bread and place it in a basket with a jar of Freezer Strawberry Preserves (page 68).

Food gifts have been an important part of Christmas for Michael since he was old enough to drive. His one chore during the season, even when he came back home to visit from Nashville, was to deliver these gifts—baskets of bread, cinnamon rolls, homemade candy.

Michael always bragged, "The people rave because they know it's something to eat from my mom."

Debbie enjoys baking for others too. So once their son, Ryan, starts to drive, Debbie and Michael are going to have him continue this tradition of delivering Christmas breads and goodies. Kimberly has kept this tradition also. One of her favorites is Hot Fudge Sauce (page 183). This is a great gift, packaged with two sundae glasses and an ice cream scoop!

Whipped Butter

1 lb. margarine   ½ cup buttermilk

To complement your homemade breads, create your own whipped butter! Place 1 pound of margarine (at room temperature) in mixer and whip until light. Add ½ cup buttermilk and continue to whip. It will take 20 to 30 minutes for this to mix well; then store in refrigerator and serve with homemade bread.

Grocery List: 1 lb. margarine, 1 qt. buttermilk

Kitchen Hint: Whipped butter and strawberry preserves are a great way to enhance good bread!

Freezer Strawberry Preserves

1 qt. strawberries, crushed   Juice of 1 lemon
4 cups sugar   1 pkg. Sure Jell

Wash jelly jars with scalding water, dry, and set aside. Measure fruit into a large bowl, adding lemon juice and sugar, measuring very carefully. Thoroughly mix and let stand 10 minutes. Mix ¾ cup water and 1 package of Sure Jell into small saucepan. Over high heat, bring to boil and boil one minute, stirring constantly. Stir Sure Jell into fruit, continuing to stir for 3 minutes. Quickly pour into prepared jars. Cover with lids and let stand at room temperature for 24 hours, then place in freezer. *Yield:* 6 jars.

Grocery List: 1 qt. fresh strawberries, 1 pkg. Sure Jell, Jelly jars

Pantry Checklist: Lemon, Sugar

Spinach-Cranberry Bread

(Debbie makes this for gifts)

2 cups fresh spinach (no stems) or
    1 pkg. (10 oz.) frozen chopped
    spinach, cooked and drained
3 cups all-purpose flour
3 eggs
1 cup vegetable oil
1¾ cups sugar

1 tsp. salt
¼ tsp. nutmeg
½ tsp. baking powder
1 tsp. baking soda
¼ tsp. cinnamon
1 cup fresh cranberries, sliced

Wash spinach; drain and chop in food processor. Beat eggs in mixing bowl. Add oil, sugar, and other dry ingredients, then spinach and cranberries. Mix well. Pour into 2 or 3 greased loaf pans and bake at 350° for 45 minutes to 1 hour.

Grocery List: Fresh or 10 oz. frozen spinach, 1 pkg. fresh cranberries

Pantry Checklist: Eggs, Oil, Sugar, Salt, Baking soda, Nutmeg, Cinnamon, Baking powder, Flour

Carrot-Lemon Bread

(Debbie's recipe)

½ medium lemon
1 cup vegetable oil
2 cups shredded carrots
1 tsp. salt
½ tsp. baking powder

3 large eggs
1¾ cups sugar
3 cups all-purpose flour
1 tsp. baking soda

Grind lemon (peel and pulp) in food processor or blender. Beat eggs in mixing bowl. Add oil and sugar. Mix well. Add carrots and lemon and blend. Sift together dry ingredients; add to liquid ingredients and mix until blended. Pour into a greased loaf pan and bake at 350° for about 1 hour.

Grocery List: 1 pkg. carrots, 1 lemon

Pantry Checklist: Eggs, Oil, Flour, Sugar, Salt, Baking soda, Baking powder

Banana Bread

(Debbie's recipe)

½ cup margarine
1 cup sugar
1 egg, beaten
½ tsp. baking soda
3 Tbsp. milk

1 cup mashed bananas (3 ripe)
2 cups all-purpose flour
1 tsp. baking powder
½ cup chopped pecans or walnuts

Cream margarine and sugar together. Add beaten egg. Dissolve soda in milk; stir milk into bananas. Add banana mixture to sugar mixture. Combine flour and baking powder, add to sugar-banana mixture, and add nuts. Bake in a well-greased loaf pan at 350° for 1 hour and 15 minutes. Test for doneness.

Grocery List: 3 ripe bananas, 1 pkg. pecans or walnuts

Pantry Checklist: Margarine, Sugar, Eggs, Baking soda, Milk, Flour, Baking powder

People sometimes think that Michael introduced Amy Grant to our family.
Actually Debbie and Amy knew each other when they attended high school at Harpeth Hall.

Easy Banana Bread

1 cup sugar
1 tsp. baking soda
⅓ cup pecans

2 eggs
3 bananas, mashed

1 cup all-purpose flour
½ cup butter or margarine

Blend sugar and eggs together, then add remaining ingredients and beat well. Bake in greased loaf pan at 325° for 45 minutes.

Grocery List: 3 bananas, ripe, 1 small pkg. pecans

Pantry Checklist: Eggs, Sugar, Flour, Baking soda, Margarine

Children's Healthy Banana Bread

(Whitney, Anna, and Emily made banana bread,
following these simple instructions.)

3 bananas
2 cups flour
1 tsp. salt
1 tsp. baking soda
½ cup wheat germ

1 stick butter or margarine
2 eggs, beaten
1 cup apple juice concentrate
½ cup sugar or honey

Get ready: Preheat the oven to 350°. Spray a rectangular pan (loaf pan) with cooking spray and set aside. Cover your clothes with an apron or big shirt. Ask a grownup to supervise as you follow these instructions.

Gather: Large bowl, small bowl, small pan or microwave-safe dish, big spoon, rubber spatula, rectangular loaf pan, measuring cup(s), electric mixer or wire whisk.

Mash bananas in a small bowl. In a large bowl, stir: flour, salt, baking soda, wheat germ. Melt 1 stick butter in the microwave or on the stovetop. Pour melted butter into bowl with flour mixture. Add eggs, apple juice, sugar or honey, and bananas. Mix ingredients, using an electric mixer or wire whisk. Pour batter into loaf pan. Bake at 350° for 1 hour. Serve with Mimi's whipped butter (page 68).

Grocery List: 3 bananas, 1 pkg. wheat germ, 6 oz. frozen apple juice concentrate

Pantry Checklist: Flour, Salt, Baking soda, Eggs, Butter

Pumpkin Bread

2 cups sugar	1 cup oil	3 eggs
2 cups canned pumpkin	3 cups all-purpose flour	1 tsp. cloves
1 cup pecans	¾ tsp. baking soda	½ tsp. salt
1½ tsp. cinnamon	1 tsp. nutmeg	1 tsp. baking powder

Combine sugar and oil, blending well. Add eggs and beat until light and creamy; stir in pumpkin. Combine remaining ingredients; add to creamed mixture and beat until well blended. Pour into 3 greased, floured loaf pans and bake at 325° for 1 hour or until well done.

Grocery List: 1 (16 oz.) can pumpkin, 5 lbs. flour, 1 pkg. pecans

Pantry Checklist: Eggs, Oil, Cloves, Cinnamon, Nutmeg, Baking soda, Baking powder, Salt, Sugar

Spinach and Orange Bread

½ medium orange	3 eggs	1 cup oil
1¾ cups sugar	3 cups all-purpose flour	1 tsp. salt
1 tsp. baking soda	¼ tsp. nutmeg	¼ tsp. cinnamon
½ tsp. baking powder		

1 pkg. (10 oz.) frozen chopped spinach, cooked and well drained

Grind half of orange (peel and pulp) in food processor. Beat eggs in mixing bowl and add oil and sugar; mix well. Add spinach and ground orange and blend. Add dry ingredients and blend together. Pour into two greased loaf pans and bake at 350° for about 1 hour.

Grocery List: 10 oz. pkg. frozen chopped spinach, 1 orange

Pantry Checklist: Eggs, Oil, Sugar, Flour, Salt, Baking soda, Nutmeg, Cinnamon, Baking powder

Kitchen Hint: Defrost frozen spinach in the microwave.

Mexican Corn Bread

2 cups self-rising cornmeal
1 tsp. sugar
1 green pepper, chopped
⅔ cup oil
1 small can green chilies,
   chopped and drained

1 medium onion, chopped
1 cup shredded sharp cheddar cheese
1 cup buttermilk
1 can (8½ oz.) cream-style corn
½ tsp. cayenne pepper, optional
3 eggs

Mix all ingredients well and pour into a 9 x 13 baking pan. Bake at 400° for 45 minutes.

Grocery List: 1 small pkg. self-rising cornmeal, 1 pkg. sharp cheddar cheese, 1 green pepper, 1 qt. buttermilk, 1 small can (8½ oz.) cream-style corn, 1 small can green chilies, chopped

Pantry Checklist: Eggs, Sugar, Oil, Cayenne pepper, Onion

Basic Roll Dough

1 pkg. dry yeast
⅓ cup sugar
½ cup cold water
3 cups all-purpose flour

1 tsp. sugar
½ cup shortening
1 egg

½ cup warm water
½ cup boiling water
1 tsp. salt

Cover yeast and 1 teaspoon sugar with ½ cup warm water and let sit for about 5 minutes. Blend ⅓ cup sugar and shortening with a spatula, then pour boiling water over and stir until melted. Add ½ cup cold water, yeast mixture, beaten egg, salt, and flour (1 cup at a time). Refrigerate overnight or at least 2 hours.

Roll out dough on a well-floured surface and spread with soft butter. Roll up, jelly-roll fashion, and slice about ¾ inch thick and place in muffin tins. Let rise until doubled and bake at 350° for about 10 minutes or until browned.

Grocery List: 1 pkg. dry yeast, Flour

Pantry Checklist: Sugar, Shortening, Eggs, Salt

Note: For a luncheon, bake rolls in miniature muffin tins. You can be creative with this recipe: again, use miniature muffin tins. Instead of rolling out dough, just form a ball and place a cube of cheese in the middle or a toasted pecan half.

Angel Biscuits

5 cups all-purpose flour	1 tsp. salt	1 tsp. baking soda
3 tsp. baking powder	2 to 4 Tbsp. sugar	¾ to 1 cup shortening
1 pkg. dry yeast	½ cup warm water	2 cups buttermilk

Mix dry ingredients and cut in shortening until well mixed; make well in center. Add yeast, which has been dissolved in warm water, and buttermilk. Mix well; roll out, and cut out biscuits. You may refrigerate them overnight. Bake at 400° until brown (about 10 minutes).

Grocery List: 5 lbs. flour, 2 pkgs. dry yeast, 1 can shortening, 1 qt. buttermilk

Pantry Checklist: Salt, Baking soda, Baking powder, Sugar

Cloverleaf Rolls or Loaf Bread

(Grandchildren's favorite)

½ cup sugar	½ cup oil
1 Tbsp. salt	5 to 6 cups all-purpose flour
3 cups hot water	2 pkgs. quick-rise yeast

Mix first 4 ingredients and 2 cups flour in large mixer (using dough hook). Add 1 cup flour and then yeast, using mixer. Continue adding flour gradually until dough no longer has a shine. Place in large well-greased bowl, turning once so all sides are greased. Let rise until doubled. Punch down and make into cloverleaf rolls (put 3 balls of dough in each cup of a muffin tin) or loaves of bread; let rise until doubled. Bake at 350° about 10 minutes for rolls or 15 to 20 minutes for bread.

Grocery List: 2 pkg. quick-rise yeast, 5 lbs. flour

Pantry Checklist: Salt, Sugar, Oil

Dinner Rolls

2 pkgs. yeast	½ cup warm water	5 to 6 cups flour
1 tsp. sugar	1½ cups boiling water	
½ cup sugar	1 tsp. salt	
¼ cup shortening	1 egg	

Mix yeast, ½ cup warm water, and 1 teaspoon sugar; set aside for 5 minutes. Pour 1½ cups boiling water over sugar, salt, and shortening; cool to lukewarm. Add yeast, egg, and flour. Refrigerate at least 2 hours. Shape into cloverleaf rolls and place in greased muffin pans. Let rise until doubled. Bake at 350° for 10 minutes or until brown.

Grocery List: 2 pkgs. dry yeast, 5 lbs. flour

Pantry Checklist: Salt, Sugar, Eggs, Shortening

French Bread

2½ cups warm water	1 Tbsp. salt
2 pkgs. quick-rise yeast	1 Tbsp. melted margarine
6 ½ to 7 cups all-purpose flour, unsifted	

Combine water, salt, and margarine. Beat in yeast and half of the flour. Add rest of the flour. Dough will be sticky. Let rise in an oiled, covered pan for 1 hour. Turn out on board and knead; divide into 2 parts. Shape into loaves.

Grocery List: 2 pkgs. quick-rise dry yeast, 5 lbs. flour

Pantry Checklist: Salt, Margarine

Kitchen Hint: Cover rising dough with waxed paper (coated with vegetable spray) to prevent sticking. Allow kneaded dough to rest, covered with a cloth or bowl, for 10 to 15 minutes before shaping or rolling.

Vasilopeta (Greek New Year Bread) ———

2 pkgs. active dry yeast
1½ tsp. lemon peel, grated
1 tsp. crushed anise seed
1 tsp. salt

5½ to 6 cups sifted
  all-purpose flour
1½ cups milk
3 eggs

6 Tbsp. butter or
  margarine
⅓ cup sugar

In large mixing bowl, combine yeast, 2 cups flour, lemon peel, and anise seed. Heat milk, butter, sugar, and salt just until warm, stirring occasionally to melt butter. Add to dry ingredients; then add 3 eggs. Beat at low speed for half a minute, scraping sides of bowl. Beat 3 minutes at high speed. By hand, stir in enough remaining flour to make a moderately stiff dough. Turn out onto lightly floured surface; knead till smooth and satiny, 8 to 10 minutes. Shape into ball; place in lightly greased bowl, turning once. Cover and let rise until double, 1 to 1½ hours.

Punch down. Cover and let rest 10 minutes. Shape dough into a round loaf; sprinkle with sesame seeds. Let rise until double, 30 to 45 minutes. Bake at 375° for 25 minutes.

Grocery List:

2 pkgs. dry yeast, 5 lbs. all-purpose flour, 1 lemon, Anise seed (spice section)

Pantry Checklist:

Eggs, Milk, Butter, Sugar, Salt

Kitchen Hint:

Before baking, brush yeast breads with one of the following glazes:
for a rich brown crust—1 egg yolk beaten with 1 to 2 tablespoons water
for a hard crust—1 egg white beaten with 1 to 2 tablespoons water
for a shiny brown crust—1 whole egg beaten with 1 to 2 tablespoons milk or water
for a soft crust—1 egg yolk beaten with 3 tablespoons milk or water and 2 tablespoons sugar

Portuguese Sweet Bread

½ cup sugar
1 cup hot milk
1 cup warm water

½ cup shortening
2 eggs, beaten
2 tsp. salt

6 to 6½ cups a
   all-purpose flour
2 pkgs. active dry yeast

Place sugar, shortening, and salt in large mixing bowl. Add hot milk and stir to soften shortening; cool. Beat in eggs. Soften yeast in the warm water; stir into shortening mixture. Add 4 cups of the flour; beat until smooth. Add enough of the remaining flour to make a soft dough. Turn out onto floured surface; knead until smooth. Place in greased bowl, turning once to grease surface. Cover; let rise in warm place until double, about 1¼ hours. Punch down; let rest 10 minutes, then divide dough into halves or thirds. Shape into loaves. Place in 2 greased loaf pans. Let rise until double, 45 to 60 minutes. Bake at 400° for 25 minutes.

For pan rolls: After first rising, shape dough into 36 rolls. Place in 2 greased 9 x 13 baking pans. Let rise until double, 45 minutes to 1 hour. Bake at 400° for 15 to 20 minutes.

Grocery List: 2 pkgs. dry yeast, 5 lbs. flour

Pantry Checklist: Sugar, Shortening, Salt, Eggs, Milk

Onion Rye Bread

1 pkg. dry yeast
1 Tbsp. sugar
¼ cup hot water (120°)
1½ cups all-purpose flour

2 tsp. salt
1½ Tbsp. sugar
⅔ cup rye flour
2 Tbsp. oil

⅔ cup hot milk (120°)
1 Tbsp. caraway seeds
⅓ cup onion,
   finely chopped

Combine yeast, 1 Tbsp. sugar, and ¼ cup hot water; stir until dissolved. Sift dry ingredients; add milk, oil, and yeast mixture. Mix well; add onions and caraway. Place dough in oiled bowl. Allow to rise in a warm place until doubled (about 45 minutes). Punch down and shape. Let rise until doubled. Bake at 400° for 10 minutes if making rolls, or for 30 to 35 minutes if making loaves.

Grocery List: 1 pkg. dry yeast, 1 lb. rye flour, Caraway seeds (spice section)

Pantry Checklist: Sugar, Salt, Milk, Oil, Flour, Onions

Dilly Bread

1 pkg. dry yeast	¼ cup warm water
1 cup cottage cheese	¼ cup shortening
1 Tbsp. sugar	1 Tbsp. minced onion
2 tsp. dill seed	1 tsp. salt
¼ tsp. baking soda	1 egg, well beaten
2¼ to 2½ cups flour	Butter, melted

Soften yeast in warm water. In saucepan, heat cottage cheese to lukewarm. Stir in shortening, sugar, onion, dill seed, salt, baking soda, and yeast. Beat in egg. Add flour, a little at a time, stirring to make a soft dough. Knead on lightly floured surface until smooth and elastic, about 5 minutes. Place in greased bowl, turning once to grease surface. Cover; let rise in warm place 1 hour. Punch down; cover. Let rest 10 minutes. Shape into loaf and place in greased loaf pan. Cover; let rise again until almost double, 30 to 45 minutes. Bake at 350° for 40 minutes. Brush top with melted butter.

Grocery List: 1 pkg. dry yeast, 1 small cottage cheese, Dill seed (spice section)

Pantry Checklist: Shortening, Salt, Butter, Sugar, Minced onion, Baking soda, Egg, Flour

Michael and Ryan, age four, on a make-believe hunting expedition

Salads

Michael in his early concert days

$\mathcal{P}$LAN YOUR SALAD TO COMPLEMENT YOUR MENU. For example, if you were going to serve sesame chicken with sweet-and-sour sauce, you should plan to have a green salad rather than a sweet gelatin salad.

When Michael was growing up, he wouldn't even consider eating a salad. Then he moved to Nashville, and one of his favorite places to eat was O'Charley's. He would always order a lettuce wedge with no dressing. Finally, he has learned to eat a vegetable salad with honey mustard dressing on the side, and also Caesar salad.

Debbie loves salad. When we eat out, she usually orders a salad for the main course. Most green salads include lots of healthy fresh vegetables.

Frozen Strawberry-Pineapple Salad

1 pkg. (8 oz.) cream cheese
1 carton (8 oz.) whipped topping
1 small can (14 oz.) crushed
   pineapple, undrained

½ cup sugar
2 bananas, sliced
1 pkg. (10 oz.) frozen
   strawberries, crushed

Mix cream cheese and sugar well; add whipped topping. Fold in pineapple, strawberries, and sliced bananas and freeze in oblong dish.

Grocery List: 8 oz. cream cheese, 8 oz. whipped topping, 1 small can (14 oz.) crushed pineapple, 10 oz. frozen sliced strawberries, 2 bananas

Pantry Checklist: Sugar

Note: To reduce fat in this recipe, use fat-free or low-fat cream cheese; to reduce sugar, use 8 or 9 packages artificial sweetener.

Frozen Strawberry Salad

1 pkg. (10 oz.) frozen strawberries
1 can (14 oz.) condensed milk

1 can (14 oz.) crushed pineapple
1 carton (14 oz.) whipped topping

Mix all ingredients. Freeze in 9 x 13 pan. Cut into squares and garnish with fresh strawberries or Party Salad Topping.

Party Salad Topping:
1 carton (4½ oz.) whipped topping
¼ cup Tang powdered drink mix

¼ cup mayonnaise

Mix well and refrigerate until serving time.

Grocery List: 10 oz. frozen sliced strawberries, 14-oz. can crushed pineapple, 14-oz. can sweetened condensed milk, 1 large and 1 small carton whipped topping, 1 jar Tang

Pantry Checklist: Mayonnaise

Note: To reduce fat, use fat-free condensed milk.

Cranberry Gelatin Mold

2 pkgs. (3 oz. each) raspberry gelatin
1 can (16 oz.) cranberry sauce or
   relish with grated orange
¾ cup apple, chopped

1 small can (14 oz.) crushed pineapple
½ cup celery, finely diced
¼ cup chopped pecans

Prepare gelatin as directed, using 1½ cups boiling water. Add cranberry sauce, then pineapple, to hot mixture. Place bowl in refrigerator until mixture begins to jell. Remove and add celery, apple, and pecans. Spoon into 10-inch ring mold or oblong glass dish and chill.

Grocery List: 2 pkgs. (3 oz. each) raspberry gelatin, 1 small can crushed pineapple,
                    1 jar cranberry relish or sauce, 1 pkg. celery, 2 apples, 1 pkg. pecans

Tangy Lemon-Lime Salad

1 pkg. (3 oz.) lemon gelatin
1 cup boiling water
1 cup sour cream
¾ cup celery, finely diced
½ cup chopped pecans

1 pkg. (3 oz.) lime gelatin
1 cup mayonnaise
1 cup small-curd cottage cheese
1 can (8¼ oz.) crushed pineapple
¼ cup chopped pimientos

Dissolve gelatin in boiling water. Combine remaining ingredients in a large bowl; mix well. Stir in hot gelatin, blending thoroughly. Pour into 2-quart mold and chill until set.

Grocery List: 1 pkg. (3 oz.) each lemon and lime gelatin, 1 pt. sour cream, 1 small
                    cottage cheese, 1 pkg. celery, 1 small can crushed pineapple,
                    1 pkg. pecans, 1 jar pimientos

Pantry Checklist: Mayonnaise

Kitchen Hint: If you wet the dish on which the gelatin salad is to be
                    unmolded, it can be moved around until centered.

Strawberry Pretzel Salad

2 Tbsp. sugar   2 cups crushed pretzels   ¾ cup melted butter

Mix and place in 9 x 13 pan. Bake at 375° for 8 minutes, then cool in freezer.

1 cup sugar   1 pkg. (8 oz.) cream cheese
1 carton (8 oz.) whipped topping   1 carton (10 oz.) frozen strawberries
2 cups boiling water   1 large pkg. (6 oz.) strawberry gelatin

Cream together sugar and cream cheese, add whipped topping, and mix well. Spread over pretzel mixture in 9 x 13 pan; place in refrigerator until cold. In a medium mixing bowl, mix boiling water with strawberry gelatin; stir until dissolved. Add frozen strawberries; put gelatin mixture in refrigerator or freezer until it begins to thicken, then pour over cream cheese mixture.

Grocery List: 1 bag pretzels, 8 oz. cream cheese, 8 oz. whipped topping, 10 oz. frozen strawberries, 1 large pkg. strawberry gelatin

Pantry Checklist: Sugar, Butter

Frozen Cherry Salad

1 can (16 oz.) cherry pie filling   1 can (14 oz.) crushed pineapple
1 can (14 oz.) sweetened condensed milk   1 carton (13 oz.) whipped topping

Mix the above ingredients and freeze. Serve with topping below.

Topping:
1 cup whipped topping   ¼ cup mayonnaise   ¼ cup Tang powder

Mix well. Refrigerate until ready to serve.

Grocery List: 1 can cherry pie filling, 1 can (14 oz.) crushed pineapple, 1 can sweetened condensed milk, 1 large and 1 small whipped topping, 1 jar Tang

Pantry Checklist: Mayonnaise

Lime Dessert Salad

2 pkgs. (3 oz.) lime gelatin
1½ cups Sprite or ginger ale
2 cups crushed pineapple,
   drained (reserve syrup)
2 eggs, lightly beaten
½ cup shredded cheddar cheese

2 cups boiling water
2 bananas
½ cup sugar
2 Tbsp. flour
1 carton (12 oz.) whipped topping

Dissolve gelatin in boiling water. Add Sprite, bananas, and crushed pineapple. Pour into 9 x 13 dish and chill until set. Mix sugar, flour, reserved pineapple juice, and eggs in small saucepan. Cook until thickened. Cool completely and add whipped topping. Spread on top of salad and sprinkle with cheese.

Grocery List: 2 small pkgs. lime gelatin, 1 can (12 oz.) Sprite or ginger ale, 1 large can crushed pineapple, 12 oz. whipped topping, 1 pkg. shredded cheddar cheese, 2 bananas

Pantry Checklist: Sugar, Flour, Eggs

Kitchen Hint: To ease unmolding and serving of gelatin salads, spray the mold or dish with cooking spray.

Lemon Pineapple Salad

1 pkg. (3 oz.) lemon gelatin
1¼ cups ginger ale
¼ cup white seedless grapes, halved

¾ cup boiling water
¼ cup celery, chopped
1 can (11 oz.) pineapple tidbits,
   drained

Dissolve gelatin in boiling water. Add ginger ale and chill until it begins to thicken. Add remaining ingredients and chill until firm.

Grocery List: 1 small pkg. lemon gelatin, 1 pkg. white grapes, 1 can pineapple tidbits, 1 qt. ginger ale, 1 pkg. celery

Lemon Cherry Salad

1 pkg. (3 oz.) pkg. lemon gelatin
½ cup small-curd cottage cheese
½ cup chopped pecans
1 cup crushed pineapple, drained

1 cup boiling water
8 oz. whipped topping
½ cup quartered maraschino cherries

Dissolve gelatin in boiling water; chill until partially set. Fold in remaining ingredients. Pour into a 5-cup mold and chill until firm.

Grocery List: 1 small pkg. lemon gelatin, 1 small container cottage cheese, 8 oz. carton whipped topping, 1 pkg. pecans, 1 small jar maraschino cherries, 1 small can crushed pineapple

Lemon-Orange Gelatin Salad

1 pkg. (3 oz.) each orange
   and lemon gelatins
1 can (20 oz.) crushed pineapple
   (reserve juice)

1½ cups boiling water
2 cups cold water
2 bananas, sliced

Dissolve gelatin in boiling water; add cold water. Chill until mixture begins to thicken and fold in fruit.

Topping:
2 Tbsp. flour
1 egg
½ cup sugar

Reserved pineapple juice
1 carton (8 oz.)
   whipped topping

Mix first 4 ingredients together and cook until thick. Let set until cool. Mix with whipped topping and spread on top of salad.

Grocery List: 1 small pkg. each orange and lemon gelatins, 1 large can crushed pineapple, 2 bananas, 8 oz. whipped topping

Pantry Checklist: Flour, Sugar, Eggs

Chicken Salad with Grapes

6 Tbsp. lemon juice
2 cups mayonnaise
3 cups diced celery
1 cup toasted slivered almonds (optional)

2 tsp. salt
10 cups diced cooked chicken
2 cups seedless grapes, halved

Add lemon juice and salt to mayonnaise; mix well. Combine chicken, celery, and grapes. Add the mayonnaise mixture and toss lightly. Chill until ready to serve. Sprinkle with almonds.

Grocery List: 1 qt. mayonnaise, 1 pkg. slivered almonds, 6 whole chicken breasts, Celery, Seedless grapes

Pantry Checklist: Lemon juice, Salt

Party Chicken Salad

10 lbs. chicken breasts, cooked
2 Tbsp. lemon juice
¼ cup half-and-half
4 cups white seedless grapes, halved

4 cups celery, chopped
1 qt. mayonnaise
1 Tbsp. dry mustard
2 cups toasted pecans

Cook chicken and let cool in broth. Cut up chicken breasts, mix with celery and lemon juice, and let stand for several hours. Blend mayonnaise, half-and-half, and mustard and add to chicken mixture. Add grapes and pecans just before serving. *Yield:* 25 servings.

Grocery List: 10 lbs. chicken breasts, 2 pkgs. celery, 1 qt. mayonnaise, Grapes, 1 large pkg. pecans, 1 pt. half-and-half

Pantry Checklist: Lemon juice, Salt, Dry mustard

Easy Tossed Salad

Croutons:
1 cup bread cubes or croutons   ¼ stick butter, melted   1 tsp. garlic salt

Heat the above at 325° for 1 hour.

1 head lettuce, torn   4 green onions, chopped   2 hard-boiled eggs, chopped

Dressing:
1 cup mayonnaise   1 cup Parmesan cheese   ½ cup Italian dressing

Pour dressing over salad and mix lightly. Add croutons just before serving.

Grocery List: 1 pkg. croutons, 1 head lettuce, Green onions, 1 small bottle Italian dressing, 1 jar Parmesan cheese

Pantry Checklist: Butter, Garlic salt, Eggs, Mayonnaise

Kitchen Hint: Always tear lettuce rather than cutting with a knife.

Sesame Almond Salad

1 head lettuce, torn   ¼ cup green onion, chopped
2 Tbsp. bacon bits (or 4 slices   3 oz. sliced almonds
   bacon, cooked and crumbled)   3 Tbsp. sesame seeds
½ cup chow mein noodles   1 cup red seedless grapes, sliced in half

Mix together; add dressing just before serving.

Dressing:
4 Tbsp. sugar   1 tsp. salt   ¼ tsp. pepper
⅓ cup oil   2 Tbsp. white vinegar

Mix thoroughly and refrigerate at least 2 hours. Shake well before adding to salad.

Grocery List: 1 head lettuce, Green onions, 1 jar bacon bits or fresh bacon, 1 pkg. chow mein or rice noodles, Red seedless grapes, 1 small pkg. sliced almonds, 1 jar sesame seeds (spice section)

Pantry Checklist: Oil, White vinegar, Sugar, Salt, Pepper

Layered Salad

1 head lettuce, torn into pieces
½ cup red onion, chopped
½ cup celery, chopped
1 pkg. (9 oz.) frozen peas
½ cup green pepper, chopped

Arrange in layers as listed above in a large salad bowl.

Spread over top:

2 cups mayonnaise
1 cup chow mein noodles
10 slices bacon, fried crisp and crumbled

2 Tbsp. sugar
1 cup sharp cheddar cheese, shredded

Cover and refrigerate 24 hours. Toss just before serving.

Grocery List: 1 head lettuce, 1 red onion, 1 bunch celery, 1 pkg. frozen peas,
1 green pepper, 1 pt. mayonnaise, 1 pkg. chow mein noodles,
1 pkg. shredded cheddar cheese, 1 lb. bacon

Pantry Checklist: Sugar

Carrot and Raisin Salad

3 lbs. carrots, shredded
1 medium can (15.25 oz.) pineapple
    chunks, drained
1 tsp. vanilla

1½ cups sugar
½ cup raisins
¾ tsp. lemon juice
1 cup mayonnaise

Mix together and chill until served.

Grocery List: 3 lbs. carrots, 1 medium can pineapple chunks, 1 box raisins

Pantry Checklist: Sugar, Lemon juice, Vanilla, Mayonnaise

Marinated Tomatoes

¼ cup wine vinegar
¼ tsp. salt
2 tsp. sugar
2 Tbsp. oil
½ tsp. oregano

Dash of pepper
6 tomatoes, quartered
1 green pepper, chopped
2 green onions, chopped

Mix first 6 ingredients and pour over tomatoes, onions, and peppers. Marinate several hours in refrigerator before serving.

Grocery List: 1 bottle wine vinegar, 6 tomatoes, 1 green pepper, Green onions

Pantry Checklist: Oil, Salt, Pepper, Oregano, Sugar

Broccoli Delight Salad

1 large bunch broccoli, cut into
    small pieces (4 to 5 cups)
10 strips bacon, fried crisp
    and crumbled
1 cup seedless grapes, red or white

1 cup raisins
¼ cup red onion, diced
1 cup sunflower seeds or
    toasted pecans

Dressing:
3 to 4 Tbsp. sugar
1 Tbsp. cider vinegar

½ cup light mayonnaise

Place washed, well-drained broccoli in large glass bowl. Add raisins, onion, bacon, sunflower seeds or pecans, and grapes. Mix together dressing ingredients. Pour over salad.

Grocery List: 1 bunch fresh broccoli, 1 box raisins, 1 red onion, 1 lb. bacon,
                   1 pkg. sunflower seeds or pecans, 1 bag seedless grapes

Pantry Checklist: Sugar, Mayonnaise, Vinegar

Crispy Coleslaw

1 small head cabbage, shredded (about 1½ lbs.)	½ green pepper, chopped
	½ red pepper, chopped
1 medium onion, chopped	1 cup sugar
½ cup plus 2 Tbsp. cider vinegar	½ cup vegetable oil
1 tsp. salt	1 tsp. celery seeds

Combine cabbage, peppers, onion, and sugar in a large bowl; stir well. Cover and chill 2 hours. Combine remaining ingredients in a saucepan; bring to a boil, stirring until salt dissolves. Pour over cabbage mixture; toss gently. Cover and chill at least 2 hours before serving. Will keep several days in the refrigerator. *Yield:* 6 to 8 servings.

Grocery List: 1 small head cabbage (1½ lbs.), 1 green pepper, 1 red pepper

Pantry Checklist: Sugar, Oil, Salt, Celery seeds, Vinegar, Onion

Fresh Vegetable Medley

1 lb. fresh cauliflower, cut into small pieces	1 lb. fresh broccoli, cut into small pieces
1 lb. carrots, sliced	1 jar (3.8 oz.) sliced black olives
1 pt. cherry tomatoes, halved	½ lb. fresh mushrooms, sliced
1 can (8 oz.) sliced water chestnuts	1 bottle (8 oz.) Italian salad dressing
2 pkgs. artificial sweetener	

Combine all ingredients and marinate in refrigerator 2 hours before serving.

Grocery List: 1 lb. cauliflower, 1 lb. broccoli, 1 lb. carrots, 1 pt. cherry tomatoes, ½ lb. fresh mushrooms, 1 can (8 oz.) sliced water chestnuts, 1 jar (3.8 oz.) black olives, 1 small bottle Italian salad dressing

Pantry Checklist: Artificial sweetener

Marinated Vegetable Salad

1 can (14½ oz.) French green beans
1 can (15¼ oz.) white corn
1 medium jar (4 oz.) diced pimientos
1 green pepper, chopped
1 cup vinegar
2 Tbsp. water
Pepper to taste

1 medium can (15 oz.) small peas
4 stalks celery, chopped
1 medium onion, chopped
1½ cups sugar
¼ cup oil
1 tsp. salt

Drain all vegetables and mix with celery, green pepper, and onion. Mix sugar, vinegar, oil, water, salt, and pepper in small saucepan and heat until sugar is dissolved. Mix with vegetables. Refrigerate overnight.

Grocery List: 1 can French green beans, 1 jar pimientos, 1 can peas, 1 can white corn, 1 pkg. celery, 1 green pepper

Pantry Checklist: Onion, Sugar, Vinegar, Oil, Pepper, Salt

Spaghetti Salad

1 pkg. (1 lb.) thin spaghetti,
  cooked and drained
3 green onions, chopped
1 tomato, diced
1 green pepper, diced

1 pkg. Good Seasons
  Italian dressing mix
¾ cup chopped celery
1 cucumber, diced
½ bottle salad seasoning

Mix Italian dressing according to package directions and pour over spaghetti in large bowl. Add remaining ingredients and toss together. This is better if made the day before.

Grocery List: 1 lb. thin spaghetti, 1 pkg. Good Seasons Italian dressing mix, 1 bunch celery, 1 cucumber, 1 green pepper, 1 tomato, Green onions, 1 jar salad seasoning (spice section)

Pantry Checklist: Oil, Vinegar

Spinach Orange Salad

1 pkg. fresh spinach, washed, well drained, and torn into small pieces
1 large purple onion, sliced into rings
1 can (11 oz.) mandarin oranges, drained
1 cup toasted pecans (see Kitchen Hint, page 95)

Mix all of the above in bowl.

Poppy Seed Dressing:
½ cup sugar
1 tsp. prepared mustard
¼ cup cider vinegar

⅔ cup vegetable oil
2 Tbsp. poppy seed
1 tsp. salt

Beat together well and store in jar in refrigerator. Toss with salad just before serving.

Grocery List: 1 pkg. fresh spinach, 1 purple onion, 1 can mandarin oranges, 1 pkg. pecans

Pantry Checklist: Sugar, Oil, Mustard, Poppy seed, Vinegar, Salt

Spinach Salad and Dressing

1 pkg. fresh spinach, washed, stemmed, and torn into pieces
2 hard-boiled eggs, chopped

Croutons
6 slices bacon, fried crisp and crumbled

Dressing:
1 cup vegetable oil
⅓ cup ketchup
1 Tbsp. Worcestershire sauce
Salt to taste

¼ cup sugar
¼ cup cider vinegar
1 medium onion, chopped fine

Refrigerate. When ready to serve, sprinkle bacon, eggs, and croutons over spinach; add dressing.

Grocery List: 1 bag fresh spinach, 1 lb. bacon, 1 pkg. croutons

Pantry Checklist: Sugar, Eggs, Oil, Onion, Vinegar, Salt, Ketchup, Worcestershire sauce

Raspberry Spinach Salad

1 Tbsp. raspberry vinegar
⅓ cup vegetable oil
¾ cup toasted pine nuts
1 cup fresh raspberries

2 Tbsp. raspberry jam
1 pkg. fresh spinach, rinsed, stemmed,
   and torn into pieces
3 kiwifruit, peeled and sliced

To prepare dressing, combine vinegar and jam in blender or small bowl. Add oil slowly, blending well. Toss spinach, half of pine nuts, half of raspberries, and half of kiwifruit with the dressing. Top individual salad servings with remaining nuts, raspberries, and kiwifruit. Serve immediately.

Grocery List: 1 bottle raspberry vinegar, 1 jar raspberry jam, 1 pkg. fresh spinach, 1 pkg. pine nuts, 3 kiwifruit, 1 pt. fresh raspberries

Pantry Checklist: Oil

Apple Spinach Salad

1 pkg. fresh spinach
½ red onion, sliced thin
¾ cup toasted walnuts

2 red delicious apples, sliced thin
   (do not peel)
lemon juice or clear carbonated soda

Wash and drain spinach and tear into pieces. Slice apple and rinse in clear carbonated soda or lemon juice. Slice onion. Prepare salad in individual bowls, beginning layers with spinach, then onion, apple, and walnuts. Serve with dressing.

Dressing:
1 cup oil
1 cup wine vinegar
¼ tsp. dry mustard

1 cup sugar
½ tsp. salt

Mix all dressing ingredients in a jar and shake well.

Grocery List: 1 pkg. fresh spinach, 2 apples, 1 pkg. walnuts, 1 red onion

Pantry Checklist: Sugar, Oil, Wine vinegar, Salt, Dry mustard, Lemon juice or clear soda

Strawberry Spinach Salad

1 pkg. fresh spinach
1 red onion, sliced thin

1 qt. fresh strawberries, halved
¾ cup toasted pecans

Wash and drain spinach and tear into pieces. Slice strawberries in two and slice onion thinly. Prepare salad in individual bowls, beginning with layers of spinach, then onion, strawberries, and pecans. Top with Poppy Seed Dressing (page 96).

Grocery List: 1 pkg. fresh spinach, 1 red onion, 1 qt. fresh strawberries, 1 pkg. pecans

Kitchen Hint: To toast pecans, melt, ¼ cup of butter for every cup of pecans. Toss pecans in butter, then spread in 9 x 13 pan. Bake at 300° for 10 minutes.

French Dressing

1 cup ketchup
1½ cups oil
2 Tbsp. cider vinegar
1 clove garlic

½ cup sugar
1 tsp. salt
1 onion

Place all ingredients in blender and mix well. Store in refrigerator.

Grocery List: 1 small bottle ketchup, 1 clove garlic

Pantry Checklist: Oil, Sugar, Onion, Salt, Vinegar

Poppy Seed Dressing

1 tsp. poppy seed
½ tsp. salt
½ tsp. dry mustard
1 Tbsp. lemon juice

½ cup sugar
⅓ cup cider vinegar
1 tsp. onion juice
1 cup oil

Mix poppy seed, sugar, salt, vinegar, dry mustard, onion juice, and lemon juice in blender. Slowly add oil and mix until well blended. Store in refrigerator and shake well before using.

Grocery List: 1 jar poppy seed (spice section), 1 bottle cider vinegar

Pantry Checklist: Sugar, Salt, Mustard, Onion juice, Lemon juice, Oil

Hot Bacon Dressing

8 slices bacon, cut into small pieces
½ cup cider vinegar
3 tsp. cornstarch
1 tsp. dry mustard

1¼ cups water
1½ cups sugar
½ tsp. salt

Fry bacon pieces until crisp; leave in pan undrained. In a small bowl, add water and vinegar to dry ingredients. Add to fried bacon pieces in pan and cook, stirring constantly until it thickens.

Grocery List: 1 lb. bacon, 1 bottle cider vinegar

Pantry Checklist: Sugar, Cornstarch, Dry mustard, Salt

Honey Dressing

⅔ cup sugar
1 tsp. paprika
¼ tsp. salt
⅓ cup cider vinegar
1 Tbsp. grated onion

1 tsp. dry mustard
1 tsp. celery seed
⅓ cup honey
1 Tbsp. lemon juice
1 cup vegetable oil

Mix dry ingredients. Blend in honey, vinegar, lemon juice, and onion. Add oil in slow stream, beating constantly.

Grocery List: 1 jar celery seed, 1 jar honey

Pantry Checklist: Sugar, Dry mustard, Salt, Paprika, Vinegar, Lemon juice, Oil, Onion

Sesame Seed Dressing

2 Tbsp. sesame seeds
⅓ cup oil
1 Tbsp. lemon juice
1 Tbsp. vinegar

2 Tbsp. sugar
½ clove garlic, minced
½ tsp. salt

Preheat oven to 350°. Place sesame seeds in shallow pan and bake until golden brown. Cool. Combine remaining ingredients and add sesame seeds. Cover and chill.

Grocery List: 1 jar sesame seeds, 1 clove garlic

Pantry Checklist: Oil, Lemon juice, Vinegar, Sugar, Salt

Michael and his dad after Michael appeared on the Brian Mason Show at a Nashville radio station

SOUP AND SALAD ARE A WONDERFUL COMBINATION, especially in the winter.

Here are some hints about soup:

One tablespoon flour to each cup of milk is the usual proportion for thickening cream soups. Potato soups require less flour because potatoes are a natural thickener.

If soup is too salty, add potato slices, cook a few minutes, and discard potatoes.

Always simmer soups; never boil them.

Garnishes for soups include chopped parsley or chives, sliced green onions, chopped bacon, shredded cheese, and sour cream.

You can make your own fancy croutons by cutting bread with miniature cookie cutters. Drizzle ¼ stick of butter over bread and bake at 350° for 20 minutes.

Use small kitchen appliances to simplify making soups and stews. For instance, use your blender or food processor to puree, chop, or blend foods; a food processor can slice and shred, as well. A microwave speeds preparation steps—such as melting butter, cooking onion in butter, or cooking bacon.

An electric crockery slow cooker is another natural, since it lets you start soups early in the day to be ready to serve for the evening meal. Once the food goes into the cooker, it usually cooks for several hours, depending on the recipe, and often needs no attention. You can adapt some of these methods to the recipes in this section.

Canadian Cheese Soup

¾ cup carrots, finely chopped
⅓ cup green onion, finely chopped
⅓ cup flour
2 cups milk
1½ cups shredded cheddar cheese

⅔ cup celery, finely chopped
¼ cup butter
1 can chicken broth
¼ tsp. salt

Sauté vegetables in butter until tender, but not brown. Blend in flour. Slowly stir in broth, then milk. Cook and stir until mixture boils and thickens. Add salt and cheese. Heat just until cheese melts. Serve with fresh minced parsley on top.

Grocery List: 1 pkg. carrots, 1 bunch green onions, 1 pkg. celery, 1 can chicken broth, 1 qt. milk, 1 large pkg. shredded cheddar cheese

Pantry Checklist: Butter, Flour, Salt

Easy French Onion Soup

2 large onions, thinly sliced
  and separated into rings
1 tsp. salt
3 Tbsp. all-purpose flour
1 can (14½ oz.) beef broth
Hard French bread rounds

3 Tbsp. butter or margarine, melted
1 Tbsp. oil
¼ tsp. sugar
1 can (14½ oz.) chicken broth
¼ cup cooking wine
8 slices mozzarella cheese

In a saucepan over low heat, cook onions slowly in butter and oil, covered, for 15 minutes. Stir in salt, sugar, and flour. Stir and cook a few minutes longer. Add chicken and beef broths and simmer another 15 minutes, then add cooking wine. Serve with bread rounds and cheese.

Grocery List: 2 large onions, 1 can each chicken and beef broths, 1 pkg. hard French bread rounds, 8 slices mozzarella cheese

Pantry Checklist: Margarine, Flour, Oil, Cooking wine, Sugar, Salt

Chunky Potato Soup

3 Tbsp. butter or margarine
4 cups milk
½ cup minced onion
¼ to ½ tsp. freshly ground pepper

¼ cup all-purpose flour
2 cups diced potatoes
½ to ¾ tsp. salt

Melt butter in a heavy saucepan over low heat; add flour, stirring until smooth. Cook 1 minute, stirring constantly. Gradually add milk; stir in potatoes, onion, salt, and pepper. Cook over medium heat, stirring frequently, until mixture is thickened and potatoes are done. *Yield:* 4 servings.

Grocery List: 3 large potatoes, 1 qt. milk

Pantry Checklist: Butter, Onion, Flour, Salt, Pepper

Cauliflower-Cheese Soup

4 cups cauliflower, chopped
1 tsp. soy sauce
½ tsp. garlic powder
2 Tbsp. butter
1 cup evaporated milk
1 cup shredded cheddar cheese

4 cups chicken broth
½ tsp. paprika
½ tsp. black pepper
2 Tbsp. flour
½ cup Parmesan cheese

Cook cauliflower in chicken broth with soy sauce, paprika, garlic powder, and pepper until tender. Puree in blender. Melt butter and stir in flour. Gradually add milk. Cook and stir until thickened. Add puree and cheeses. Heat well. Garnish with parsley. *Yield:* 6 servings.

Grocery List: 2 heads cauliflower, 2 cans chicken broth, 1 can evaporated milk, 1 pkg. shredded cheddar cheese, 1 jar Parmesan cheese

Pantry Checklist: Soy sauce, Paprika, Garlic powder, Pepper, Butter, Flour

Pimiento Cheese Soup

1 jar (4 oz.) pimientos, undrained
2½ Tbsp. flour
1½ cups half-and-half
½ tsp. salt

2 Tbsp. butter
1 can (14½ oz.) chicken broth
2 tsp. grated onion
¼ tsp. hot sauce

Blend pimientos in blender until smooth. Set aside. Melt butter and add flour; stir until smooth. Cook one minute, stirring constantly. Add broth and half-and-half gradually to flour mixture. Cook over medium heat, stirring constantly until thick and bubbly. Stir in pimientos, onion, salt, and hot sauce. Cook on low heat, stirring constantly.

Grocery List: 4-oz. jar pimientos, 1 can chicken broth, 1 qt. half-and-half

Pantry Checklist: Butter, Onion, Flour, Salt, Hot sauce

Asparagus Cheese Soup

¼ cup butter
2 tsp. salt
2 cans (14.5 oz.) asparagus pieces
⅛ tsp. cayenne pepper
2 Tbsp. white cooking sherry

¼ cup flour
6 cups milk
2 cups shredded cheddar cheese
⅛ tsp. nutmeg

In a 3-quart saucepan, melt butter. Stir in flour and salt and cook until smooth. Gradually add milk; bring to a boil. Boil and stir for 2 minutes. Add asparagus and heat through. Add the cheese, cayenne pepper, and nutmeg. Cook until cheese is melted, stirring frequently (do not boil), then add cooking sherry. Garnish with additional cheese if desired.

Grocery List: 2 cans asparagus pieces, 1 gal. milk, 1 large pkg. shredded
cheddar cheese

Pantry Checklist: Butter, Flour, Salt, Cayenne pepper, White cooking sherry, Nutmeg

Tomato Basil Soup

4 cups tomatoes (8 to 10 fresh), peeled,
  chopped, and cored, or 2 cans
  crushed tomatoes
1 stick unsalted butter

4 cups tomato juice
12 fresh basil leaves
1 cup lowfat canned cream
Salt and pepper to taste

Combine tomatoes and juice in saucepan. Simmer 30 minutes. Puree in blender along with basil (in small batches) or food processor. Return to saucepan and add cream, butter, and salt and pepper to taste. Continue cooking over low heat, stirring constantly until hot. Garnish with basil leaves and serve with warm bread.

 Grocery List: 2 14-oz. cans crushed tomatoes or 8 to 10 fresh tomatoes, 32-oz. can tomato juice, Fresh basil leaves, 1 can lowfat cream, Unsalted butter

Pantry Checklist: Salt, Pepper

Chicken Rice Soup

2 chicken breasts, cooked and
  chopped (reserve broth)
¼ cup chopped onion
Salt and pepper to taste

1 can chicken broth
½ cup chopped celery
¾ cup grated carrots
1½ cups cooked rice

Cook chicken breasts until tender. Reserve broth. Chop chicken. Add canned chicken broth to reserved broth and add celery, carrots, and onions. Simmer until tender. Season with salt and pepper. Add chopped chicken and rice and simmer until hot.

 Grocery List: 2 chicken breasts, 1 can chicken broth, 1 pkg. carrots, 1 pkg. celery, 1 pkg. white or brown rice

Pantry Checklist: Salt, Pepper, Onion

Vegetable Soup

3 potatoes, peeled and chopped
½ cup celery, chopped
1 cup cabbage, finely chopped
1 large can (46 oz.) tomato juice
Salt and pepper to taste

1 onion, chopped
1 tsp. instant beef bouillon
2 cups water
1 pkg. (10 oz.) frozen mixed vegetables

Cook potatoes, onion, celery, bouillon, and cabbage in water until tender. Add tomato juice, frozen vegetables, and salt and pepper. Continue to cook until vegetables are tender.

Grocery List: 3 potatoes, 1 onion, 1 pkg. celery, 1 small cabbage, 1 can (46 oz.) tomato juice, 10 oz. frozen mixed vegetables

Pantry Checklist: Salt, Pepper, Beef bouillon

Zucchini Soup

3 lbs. zucchini
1 small onion, chopped
2 cans (10¾ each) nonfat chicken broth
1½ cups half-and-half
Chopped chives

1 tsp. salt
⅛ tsp. white pepper
½ cup water
½ tsp. fresh or dried basil

Cut ends off zucchini and slice into 1-inch pieces. Place in 6-quart saucepan. Add salt, onion, white pepper, chicken broth, and water. Bring to a boil. Cover and cook over moderate heat until tender, about 10 minutes. Place ⅓ of zucchini slices and broth at a time in a blender or food processor fitted with metal blade. Blend until smooth. Place in a clean saucepan. Stir in half-and-half. Season to taste with salt, white pepper, and basil. Stir over moderate heat until heated through. Top with chives. May be refrigerated overnight.

Grocery List: 3 lbs. zucchini, 2 cans low-fat chicken broth, 1 qt. half-and-half

Pantry Checklist: Salt, White Pepper, Pepper, Onion, Basil, Chives

Broccoli Soup

2 cups milk	2 Tbsp. flour
2 Tbsp. butter	1 tsp. salt
1/8 tsp. pepper	1/2 cup shredded sharp cheddar cheese
1 pkg. (10 oz.) frozen chopped broccoli	1 Tbsp. chopped onion

Cook broccoli in microwave; drain well. Melt butter in saucepan; add flour and whisk until well mixed. Add onion, salt, pepper, and milk. Cook until mixture thickens a little, then add broccoli and cheese. Cook until cheese melts.

Grocery List: 1 qt. milk, 10 oz. pkg. frozen chopped broccoli, 1 pkg. shredded sharp cheddar cheese

Pantry Checklist: Flour, Butter, Salt, Pepper, Onion

Cream of Spinach Soup

1 pkg. (10 oz.) frozen chopped spinach	2 Tbsp. butter
1/2 cup fresh mushrooms, sliced	2 Tbsp. flour
1 Tbsp. chopped onion	1 tsp. salt
1/8 tsp. pepper	2 cups milk

Cook spinach in microwave; drain well. Melt butter in saucepan and sauté mushrooms and onions for 3 or 4 minutes. Set aside mushrooms and onions; add flour and whisk until well mixed. Add mushrooms, onion, salt, pepper, and milk. Cook until mixture thickens a little, then add spinach. Serve immediately.

Grocery List: 1 qt. milk, 1 pkg. fresh mushrooms, 10 oz. pkg. frozen chopped spinach

Pantry Checklist: Flour, Butter, Salt, Pepper, Onion

Vegetables

Michael, two and a half, with his dad before an Industrial League game. Paul played for Kemple Glass.

WHEN MICHAEL WAS A BABY, HE ATE VERY WELL. In fact, he was a chunky little guy. Then when he was about five years old, he had his tonsils removed. Oh, what a picky eater he became after that. He would not eat vegetables!

In desperation I called the pediatrician. "Dr. Parsons, Michael will not eat his squash," I said.

He replied, "Now, Mrs. Smith, don't tell me he won't eat his squash."

The doctor was sure I could change this. But nothing seemed to work, so I had to cook two meals every night. Paul, Kim, and I had dinner, and Michael had dinner. The only foods he would eat were mashed potatoes, hamburgers, pizza, hot dogs, corn chips, and white cake with white icing.

Thank goodness, Michael's eating habits have changed over the years, especially since he and Debbie married. He eats most everything and still loves to come to our house for dinner. Some of his favorite vegetables are Spinach-Cheese Soufflé (page 123), Asparagus Casserole (page 121), and Sweet Potato Casserole (page 118). So even though I can't give you hints for how to get your children to eat vegetables, I can assure you that the problem will eventually correct itself.

Debbie plans her meals very carefully; the children always have a variety, including a vegetable, pasta, and fruit, for dinner.

Pea Casserole

⅓ cup green pepper, finely chopped
1 small onion
2 cups celery, finely chopped
3 Tbsp. butter or margarine
2 cans (17 oz. each) English peas, drained

2 Tbsp. chopped pimientos
1 can (8 oz.) sliced water chestnuts
1 can cream of mushroom soup
2 Tbsp. milk
¾ cup soft bread crumbs

Sauté green pepper, onion, and celery in butter in a large saucepan until tender. Remove from heat. Add next 5 ingredients; mix well. Spoon mixture into a greased 10 x 6 x 2 baking dish; sprinkle with bread crumbs. Bake, uncovered, at 350° for 30 minutes. *Yield:* 8 servings.

Grocery List: 1 green pepper, 1 pkg. celery, 2 cans tiny English peas, 1 small jar pimientos, 1 small can water chestnuts, 1 can cream of mushroom soup

Pantry Checklist: Onion, Margarine, Milk, Soft bread crumbs

Peas Amandine

1 pkg. (16 oz.) frozen peas
3 Tbsp. butter or margarine
1 jar (4½ oz.) sliced mushrooms, drained
⅛ tsp. pepper

¼ cup slivered almonds
¼ cup onion, chopped
¼ tsp. salt
¼ cup chopped pimientos

Cook peas according to directions; drain. Set aside and keep warm. In a skillet, sauté almonds in butter until lightly browned. Remove with a slotted spoon; add to peas. In the same skillet, sauté mushrooms and onions until tender; add to peas. Season with salt and pepper and add pimientos.

Grocery List: 16-oz. pkg. frozen peas, 1 pkg. slivered almonds, 1 small jar pimientos, 1 small jar sliced mushrooms

Pantry Checklist: Margarine, Onion, Salt, Pepper

Broccoli Ritz Casserole

2 pkgs. (10 oz.) frozen broccoli spears
1 cup shredded cheddar cheese
5 Tbsp. margarine

2 Tbsp. milk
24 Ritz crackers, finely crushed

Cook broccoli spears until tender; drain and place in greased casserole dish. Pour the milk over top. Top with cheese. Melt butter and mix with Ritz crackers. Place cracker mixture on top and bake at 350° for 30 minutes.

Grocery List: 2 pkg. frozen broccoli spears, 1 pkg. shredded cheddar cheese, 1 box Ritz crackers

Pantry Checklist: Milk, Margarine

Broccoli Fromage

4 mushroom caps, sliced
2 Tbsp. flour
⅛ tsp. dry mustard
2 Tbsp. cooking sherry
¼ cup grated cheddar cheese
½ cup browned almonds

3 Tbsp. butter
½ tsp. salt
1 cup milk
1 box (10 oz.) frozen chopped
  broccoli, cooked and drained
2 Tbsp. chopped pimientos

Sauté mushrooms in butter and set aside. Add to skillet: flour, salt, and mustard and cook 1 minute; add milk and cooking sherry, and cook until thickened. Place cooked broccoli in greased 9 x 13 pan and cover with sauce, cheese, almonds, mushroom caps, and pimientos. Bake at 350° for 20 minutes.

Grocery List: 1 pkg. fresh mushrooms, 1 pkg. frozen chopped broccoli, 1 pkg. sliced almonds, 1 pkg. shredded cheddar cheese, 1 small jar pimientos, 1 bottle cooking sherry

Pantry Checklist: Butter, Flour, Milk, Salt, Dry mustard

Note: The above recipe can be used with asparagus instead of broccoli. It's great!

Kitchen Hint: Cheddar cheese grates more easily if it is placed in the freezer for 10 to 20 minutes beforehand.

Broccoli Soufflé

¼ cup melted butter
1 cup cottage cheese
1 pkg. (10 oz.) frozen chopped broccoli
2 Tbsp. flour

3 eggs, beaten
1½ cups sharp cheddar cheese, grated
½ tsp. salt

Cook broccoli in microwave for 3 minutes on high. Mix all ingredients and bake in round baking dish at 350° for 40 minutes.

Grocery List: 1 small cottage cheese, 1 pkg. shredded sharp cheddar cheese, 1 pkg. frozen chopped broccoli

Pantry Checklist: Butter, Eggs, Salt, Flour

Kitchen Hint: If using fresh broccoli, cut through stems to hasten cooking time.

Squash Casserole

½ cup margarine
2 lbs. squash, cooked and drained
1 small jar pimientos
1 (8 oz.) container sour cream

1 pkg. herb-seasoned stuffing mix
1 large onion, chopped
1 can cream of chicken soup
1 cup shredded cheese (optional)

Melt butter and add to stuffing mix. Mix remaining ingredients along with half of stuffing mixture; place in greased 9 x 13 baking dish. Top with remaining stuffing mix and bake at 350° for 45 minutes.

Grocery List: 2 lbs. squash, 1 small jar pimientos, 1 can cream of chicken soup, 1 pt. sour cream, 1 pkg. herb-seasoned stuffing mix, 1 small pkg. shredded cheese (optional)

Pantry Checklist: Onion, Margarine

Squash Soufflé

3 lbs. yellow squash, sliced
2 eggs, beaten
¾ cup cracker crumbs
½ tsp. pepper
¾ cup shredded cheddar cheese

½ cup chopped onion
½ cup butter or margarine
1 tsp. salt
3 Tbsp. chopped pimientos

Cook squash and onion until tender. Drain well and mash. Add eggs, butter, cracker crumbs, salt, pepper, pimientos, and cheese to squash; stir well. Spoon into a lightly greased 2-quart casserole. Bake, uncovered, at 350° for 20 to 30 minutes.

Grocery List: 3 lb. squash, Small box saltine crackers, 1 pkg. shredded cheddar cheese, 1 small jar pimientos

Pantry Checklist: Butter, Onion, Eggs, Salt, Pepper

Stir-Fried Zucchini Squash

1 medium onion, sliced
1 lb. zucchini, sliced
2 Tbsp. oil
Salt and pepper to taste

1 lb. squash, sliced
2 Tbsp. butter
1 tsp. sugar

Sauté onion, squash, and zucchini in butter and oil until tender. Stir in sugar, salt, and pepper.

Grocery List: 1 lb. squash, 1 lb. zucchini

Pantry Checklist: Oil, Butter, Salt, Pepper, Sugar, Onion

Note: Add a pinch (⅛ teaspoon) of baking soda to green vegetables while cooking to retain color.

Green Beans

3 lbs. green beans, fresh or frozen
⅓ cup chopped onion
3 Tbsp. butter or margarine
2 slices bacon

1 cup water
2 Tbsp. sugar
Salt and pepper to taste

Remove strings from fresh beans and wash. Snap beans into 1-inch pieces. Place in a large pan and add water, onion, butter, sugar, salt, and pepper; place bacon on top. Bring to a boil; cover, reduce heat, and cook for 1 to 1½ hours. Remove bacon and drain off excess liquid.

Grocery List: 3 lbs. green beans

Pantry Checklist: Onion, Butter, Sugar, Bacon, Salt, Pepper

Note: If you want to use canned beans, purchase 1 gallon canned beans. Open, drain well, and rinse with water. Place in large pot; add 2 cups water, ¼ cup sugar, salt and pepper to taste, ⅓ cup onion, ¼ cup oil, and 4 slices bacon on top. Bring to a boil, then reduce heat and cook for 1½ to 2 hours on low to medium heat.

Potatoes au Gratin

5 lbs. potatoes, cooked and sliced
½ cup flour
½ cup boiling water
2 cups sharp cheddar cheese
Salt and pepper to taste

½ cup butter
1 chicken bouillon cube
½ cup milk
Dash of garlic powder

Place sliced potatoes in 9 x 13 casserole dish and salt between layers. Melt butter; add flour, bouillon, water, milk, cheese, and spices. Pour over potatoes and bake at 350° for 30 minutes. *Yield:* 12 servings.

Grocery List: 5 lbs. potatoes, 1 large pkg. shredded cheddar cheese

Pantry Checklist: Butter, Flour, Chicken bouillon, Milk, Garlic powder, Salt, Pepper

Note: This recipe can be prepared ahead of time and frozen.

Hash Brown Casserole

1 pkg. (32 oz.) hash brown
   potatoes, thawed
2 cups shredded cheddar cheese
1 stick melted butter

Topping:
2 cups crushed cornflakes

2 cups sour cream
½ cup chopped onion
½ tsp. pepper
1 can cream of chicken soup

¼ stick melted butter

Mix the above ingredients and place in a 9 x 13 casserole dish, then add topping.
Bake at 350° for 45 minutes.

Grocery List: 1 pkg. frozen hash brown potatoes, 1 large sour cream, 1 large pkg.
                         shredded cheddar cheese, 1 can cream of chicken soup, 1 box cornflakes

Pantry Checklist: Butter, Pepper, Onion

Note: To reduce fat in this recipe, use diet margarine, low-fat or no-fat cream of chicken soup, and
low-fat or no-fat sour cream.

Sour Cream Potatoes

6 large potatoes
¼ cup butter or margarine
⅓ cup chopped green onion
¼ tsp. white pepper

2 cups shredded cheddar cheese
2 cups sour cream
1 tsp. salt
4 Tbsp. butter or margarine

Cook the potatoes in boiling water until tender. Drain and cool in refrigerator.
When cooled, peel and shred coarsely and mix with other ingredients. Bake at
350° for 25 minutes.

Grocery List: 6 large potatoes, 1 pkg. shredded cheddar cheese, 1 pt. sour cream,
                         green onions

Pantry Checklist: Butter, Salt, Pepper

Sweet Potato Casserole

3 cups sweet potatoes,
   cooked and mashed
½ cup melted butter

¾ cup sugar
1 tsp. vanilla
2 eggs

Mix together and place in greased casserole dish.

Top with:
1 cup light brown sugar
1 cup pecans

⅓ cup flour
⅓ cup soft butter

Mix with fork and sprinkle on top of sweet potatoes. Bake at 350° for 40 minutes.

Grocery List: 4 to 5 sweet potatoes, 1 pkg. pecans

Pantry Checklist: Sugar, Butter, Vanilla, Eggs, Brown sugar, Flour

---

Sweet Potato Crisp

3 cups sweet potatoes, cooked and mashed
2 tsp. baking powder
¼ tsp. salt
3 eggs

1¼ cups sugar
1 tsp. vanilla
½ cup soft butter

Mix potatoes with rest of ingredients and bake at 400° until set, about 30 minutes.

Topping:
⅔ stick butter
½ cup brown sugar

3 cups cornflakes, crushed
½ cup pecans, chopped

Mix above ingredients and place on top of casserole; continue to bake 15 minutes.

Grocery List: 4 to 5 sweet potatoes, 1 box cornflakes

Pantry Checklist: Sugar, Baking powder, Salt, Vanilla, Butter, Eggs, Brown sugar,
Pecans

Sweet Potato Puffs

5 to 6 large sweet potatoes
½ cup butter
Large marshmallows

Sugar to taste
1 tsp. vanilla
Cornflakes

Boil sweet potatoes until tender. Add sugar, butter, and vanilla. Mix and place in refrigerator overnight. Next day, roll marshmallows in cold sweet potatoes, then in cornflakes. Place balls on greased baking sheet and heat at 350° for 30 minutes.

Grocery List: 5 to 6 sweet potatoes, 1 pkg. large marshmallows, 1 box cornflakes

Pantry Checklist: Sugar, Butter, Vanilla

Twice-Baked Potatoes

4 medium baking potatoes
½ cup sour cream
¼ cup butter
¾ tsp. salt

Vegetable oil
¼ cup milk
¼ cup shredded cheddar cheese
Dash of pepper

Wash potatoes, and rub skins with oil. Bake at 400° for 1 hour or until done. When potatoes cool, slice in half and scoop out pulp, leaving shells intact. Combine potato pulp and remaining ingredients in mixer and beat until well mixed. Fill potato skins with mixture and top with extra cheese. Bake at 400° for 15 minutes or until hot.

Grocery List: 4 baking potatoes, 1 pt. sour cream, 1 pkg. shredded cheddar cheese

Pantry Checklist: Oil, Milk, Salt, Pepper, Butter

Note: This could be done the day before; just remember to bake longer if made ahead.

Kitchen Hint: Cutting a thin slice from each end of the potato will speed baking time.

Vegetables

Cheese Potatoes

2 pkgs. (24 oz. each) shredded
  hash browns, thawed
1 can cream of chicken soup
1 pt. sour cream
½ cup margarine, melted

½ cup finely chopped onion
1 cup shredded cheddar cheese
Salt and pepper to taste
1 cup Ritz cracker crumbs

Mix all ingredients except cracker crumbs and place in 9 x 13 casserole dish. Place cracker crumbs on top and bake at 350° for 1 hour.

Grocery List: 2 pkgs. (24 oz. each) hash browns, 1 can cream of chicken soup, 1 pkg. shredded cheddar cheese, 1 pt. sour cream, 1 box Ritz crackers

Pantry Checklist: Margarine, Onion

Mashed Potatoes

10 medium potatoes
½ cup sour cream
2 tsp. salt

½ cup butter
¼ cup milk (or more)
¼ tsp. white pepper

Cook potatoes (cut into quarters) until well done and drain. Place in mixer with butter and mix; then add sour cream, milk, salt, and pepper. Whip until light and fluffy.

Grocery List: 10 potatoes, 1 pt. sour cream

Pantry Checklist: Butter, Milk, Salt, White pepper

Note: These potatoes can be made an hour or so ahead of serving time and reheated in microwave.

Asparagus Casserole

2 Tbsp. butter
2 Tbsp. asparagus juice
Salt and pepper to taste
Dash of paprika
1 small can (4 oz.) sliced mushrooms
3 hard-boiled eggs, sliced

2 Tbsp. flour
1 scant cup light cream
Dash of cayenne
¾ cup sharp cheddar cheese, shredded
2 cans (15 oz.) asparagus
½ cup almonds, sliced

Melt butter; add flour and blend well. Add asparagus juice; blend in cream and seasonings. Add cheese and stir until melted. Add mushrooms. Layer half of asparagus in bottom of casserole, then half of sliced eggs and half of sauce. Repeat and sprinkle almonds on top. Bake at 325° for 45 minutes.

Grocery List: 2 cans asparagus spears, 1 small can mushrooms, 1 pt. light cream, 1 pkg. shredded sharp cheddar cheese, 1 small pkg. sliced almonds

Pantry Checklist: Butter, Flour, Eggs, Salt, Pepper, Cayenne pepper, Paprika

Corn Pudding

6 ears of corn, cut off cob or
  2 10-oz. pkgs. frozen corn
3 Tbsp. flour
½ cup sugar

Salt to taste
3 Tbsp. melted butter
3 eggs, beaten
1½ cups milk

Mix all ingredients well. Pour into a lightly buttered baking dish and bake at 350° for 30 to 40 minutes. Stir once thoroughly at the end of 15 minutes.

Grocery List: 6 ears corn or 2 10-oz. pkgs. frozen corn

Pantry Checklist: Butter, Flour, Eggs, Sugar, Milk, Salt

Spinach Casserole

¼ cup butter
½ tsp. salt
1 cup sharp cheddar cheese, grated
1 pkg. (10 oz.) frozen chopped spinach,
   cooked and drained

¼ cup flour
Dash of pepper
¾ cup milk
2 Tbsp. chopped onion
4 eggs, separated

Combine butter and flour in large saucepan over low heat. Stir until smooth and bubbly. Add salt, pepper, cheese, and milk. Stir constantly over moderate heat until cheese is melted. Remove from heat. Add spinach and onion. Gradually add egg yolks, mixing well. Cool. Beat egg whites until stiff. Fold egg whites into spinach mixture. Pour into lightly greased 2-quart soufflé dish and bake at 350° for 35 minutes.

Grocery List: 1 pkg. shredded cheddar cheese, 1 box frozen chopped spinach

Pantry Checklist: Butter, Flour, Salt, Onions, Pepper, Milk, Eggs

Spinach Supreme

2 pkgs. (10 oz. each) frozen
   chopped spinach
2 eggs
1 cup grated cheddar cheese
1 can cream of mushroom soup

1 cup mayonnaise
2 small onions, chopped
¼ stick butter
¼ cup Pepperidge Farm
   cornbread stuffing mix

Cook spinach according to directions and drain thoroughly. Mix spinach, soup, mayonnaise, eggs, onions, and cheese together and place in casserole dish. Mix stuffing mix and butter and place on top. Bake at 350° for 45 minutes.

Grocery List: 2 pkgs. frozen chopped spinach, 1 can cream of mushroom soup, 1 small pkg. shredded cheese, 1 pkg. Pepperidge Farm cornbread stuffing mix

Pantry Checklist: Mayonnaise, Onions, Butter, Eggs

Spinach-Cheese Soufflé

¼ cup melted butter
1 cup small-curd cottage cheese
1 pkg. (10 oz.) frozen chopped
  spinach, cooked and drained

3 eggs, beaten
1½ cups sharp cheddar cheese, shredded
½ tsp. salt
2 Tbsp. flour

Mix all ingredients. Bake in glass dish (sprayed with cooking spray) at 350° for 40 minutes.

Grocery List: 1 small carton cottage cheese, 1 pkg. sharp cheddar cheese, 1 box frozen chopped spinach

Pantry Checklist: Butter, Flour, Salt, Eggs

Note: This is also good with Monterey Jack cheese.

Spinach Cakes

2 Tbsp. butter
1 small clove garlic, minced
½ cup milk
½ tsp. salt
⅛ tsp. nutmeg
Dash of white pepper
¼ cup grated plain bread crumbs
2 Tbsp. flour
2 Tbsp. vegetable oil

¼ cup chopped onion
3 Tbsp. flour
1 pkg. (10 oz.) frozen chopped
  spinach, cooked and drained
⅛ tsp. paprika
Dash of red pepper
2 Tbsp. Parmesan cheese
⅓ cup Pepperidge Farm cornbread
  dressing, crushed finely

In medium saucepan, melt butter over medium heat. Add onion and garlic; cook for several minutes. Add flour and cook until mixture browns, then add milk and stir with wire whisk until it begins to thicken. Stir in spinach, salt, nutmeg, paprika, white pepper, and red pepper. Remove from heat; stir in bread crumbs and Parmesan. Let mixture cool enough to handle. Meanwhile, mix flour and cornbread dressing. Shape spinach mixture into small cakes, dip in cornbread and flour mixture, and cook in vegetable oil in skillet until brown on both sides.

Grocery List: 1 pkg. (10 oz.) frozen chopped spinach, 1 box bread crumbs, 1 pkg. Pepperidge Farm cornbread dressing mix

Pantry Checklist: Butter, Flour, Onion, Garlic, Milk, Salt, Nutmeg, Paprika, White pepper, Red pepper, Parmesan cheese, Oil

Carrot Pecan Casserole

3 lbs. carrots, sliced and cooked
½ cup butter
¼ cup milk
3 Tbsp. all-purpose flour
¼ tsp. nutmeg

⅔ cup sugar
½ cup chopped pecans, toasted
2 eggs, lightly beaten
1 tsp. vanilla

Mash carrots in mixer; stir in sugar and remaining ingredients. Spoon into lightly greased casserole dish and bake at 350° for 40 minutes.

Grocery List: 3 lbs. carrots, 1 pkg. pecans

Pantry Checklist: Sugar, Butter, Milk, Eggs, Flour, Vanilla, Nutmeg

Carrot Casserole

2 cups carrots, cooked and mashed
2 Tbsp. all-purpose flour
½ cup margarine, melted
¼ tsp. cinnamon

1 cup sugar
1 tsp. baking powder
3 eggs, beaten

Mix well and pour into casserole dish. Bake at 350° for 30 to 40 minutes.

Grocery List: 1 pkg. carrots

Pantry Checklist: Sugar, Flour, Baking powder, Margarine, Cinnamon, Eggs

Main Dishes

Michael sang for President George Bush and his family at a Christmas chapel at Camp David.

*T*RY NOT TO HANDLE FOOD TOO MANY TIMES. I usually buy extra chicken so I can prepare some dishes in advance. When I prepare a chicken dish for Paul and me, I also cook enough chicken for at least two casseroles. Chicken can be stewed or cooked in the microwave, then chopped. Measure the chopped chicken by the cup and store it in the freezer for casseroles.

Some of our favorites are Cranberry Chicken (page 138), Chicken Dressing Casserole (page 139), and Sesame Chicken (page 133), one of Michael's favorites and probably one of the most popular recipes I have prepared in all of my years of catering. It takes a little preparation time, but it is worth the time and effort.

When preparing ground beef, plan to take several hours and make several dishes for the freezer such as spaghetti sauce, meat loaf, taco meat, or other favorites. Preparing several entrées at one time doesn't take as long as you might think. To feed a family of four, you could come up with three or four meals in just a couple of hours.

I cook more chicken than I do beef, but we love tenderloin. When I order tenderloin from the meat department, I always ask them to trim it and grind the trimmings. This way I get full use of whatever I pay for. I use the trimmings to make Special Spaghetti Sauce (page 141).

If you're having guests and you want to prepare early in the day, serve Eye of Round Roast (page 145). I bake this roast for several hours, and it is great served with Mashed Potatoes (page 120), which can be prepared at least 1½ hours ahead of time. I also often serve Broccoli Ritz Casserole (page 113), which can be prepared that morning.

This Main Dishes section also includes a simple Ham Loaf recipe (page 140), which is good served with sweet potatoes and a green vegetable.

To-Do List When Planning for Dinner Guests

- ☐ Choose menu.

- ☐ Study recipes. Make and organize your grocery list in the order of the floor plan of your favorite grocery store. This saves a lot of time.

- ☐ Check recipes and prepare everything possible in advance.

- ☐ Set your table the night before.

- ☐ Always have your dishwasher free and your sink empty before guests arrive.

Creamy Baked Chicken Breasts

8 chicken breast halves, skinned
1 can cream of chicken soup
1 cup herb-seasoned stuffing mix, crushed

8 slices Swiss cheese
¼ cup white cooking wine
¼ cup butter, melted

Arrange chicken in a lightly greased casserole dish; top with cheese. Combine soup and cooking wine; stir well and spoon over chicken. Top with stuffing mix, then drizzle with melted butter. Bake at 350° for 45 to 55 minutes.

Grocery List: 8 chicken breast halves, 8 slices Swiss cheese, 1 can cream of chicken soup, 1 pkg. stuffing mix

Pantry Checklist: Cooking wine, Butter

Parmesan Chicken

(Debbie's favorite chicken recipe)

½ cup butter
⅓ cup Parmesan cheese
4 chicken breasts

½ tsp. garlic salt
1 cup cornflake crumbs
(bread crumbs or dressing mix)

Melt butter and mix with garlic salt. Mix cheese and crumbs. Dip chicken in butter-garlic mixture, roll in crumbs, and place in greased baking dish. Bake at 350° for 1 hour.

Grocery List: — 1 jar Parmesan cheese, 4 chicken breasts, Cornflakes or dressing mix

Pantry Checklist: — Butter, Garlic salt

Kitchen Hint: — Six chicken breast halves equal 2⅔ cups diced, cooked chicken.

Chicken Salad

6 large chicken breast halves
2 Tbsp. vinegar
1 cup sour cream
1 cup chopped celery
½ cup sweet pickle cubes

Salt and pepper to taste
¼ cup sugar
½ cup (or more) mayonnaise
1 Tbsp. minced onion
¼ cup pimientos

Cook chicken breasts and cut into small pieces. Mix other ingredients with chicken. You may need to vary the amount of mayonnaise according to the size of the chicken breasts.

Grocery List: — 6 chicken breast halves, 1 pt. sour cream, 1 bunch celery, 1 jar sweet pickles, 1 jar pimientos

Pantry Checklist: — Salt, Pepper, Mayonnaise, Vinegar, Minced onion, Sugar

Note: This recipe is best if mixed while chicken is still warm.

Chicken Biscuits

(Paul's favorite)

2 whole chicken breasts, cooked
   and chopped (reserve broth)
1 can refrigerated flaky biscuits, baked

3 Tbsp. cornstarch
Salt and pepper to taste

Add enough water to reserved broth to make 2 cups liquid and heat. Dissolve cornstarch in ¼ cup water and add to broth; cook until gravy is right consistency. Add salt, pepper, and chicken. Serve over biscuits.

Grocery List: 2 whole chicken breasts, 1 can refrigerated flaky biscuits

Pantry Checklist: Cornstarch, Salt, Pepper

Chicken Spinach Casserole

6 slices bacon
1½ cups cooked regular rice
1 jar (2 oz.) pimientos, drained
¼ cup water chestnuts, sliced
1 can cream of mushroom soup
¾ cup light sour cream
¾ cup soft bread crumbs

½ cup chopped onion
1 pkg. (10 oz.) frozen chopped
   spinach, cooked and drained
¼ tsp. salt
¼ cup water
2 cups chicken, cooked and chopped
1 Tbsp. butter, melted

Cook bacon in a large skillet until crisp; remove bacon, reserving 2 tablespoons drippings in skillet. Crumble bacon and set aside. Sauté onion in bacon drippings until tender; remove from heat. Add rice, spinach, pimientos, water chestnuts, half of bacon, and salt; stir well. Combine soup, water, and sour cream; stir half of soup mixture into spinach mixture and place in 9 x 13 inch baking dish. Place chicken on top of spinach mixture. Spoon remaining soup mixture on top. Mix butter and bread crumbs and sprinkle around edges of casserole. Sprinkle remaining bacon in center. Bake, uncovered, at 350° for 30 minutes.

Grocery List: 6 chicken breast halves, 1 lb. bacon, 10 oz. frozen chopped spinach,
                     1 pt. sour cream, 1 small can water chestnuts, 1 can cream of
                     mushroom soup, 1 jar chopped pimientos

Pantry Checklist: Onion, Rice, Salt, Butter, Bread crumbs

Apricot Nectar Chicken

8 boneless chicken breast halves
1 can (12 oz.) apricot nectar
1 tsp. ground allspice
½ tsp. salt

¼ tsp. ginger
¼ tsp. pepper
¾ cup apricot preserves
½ cup chopped pecans, toasted

Place chicken breasts in a large baking dish. Combine apricot nectar and next 4 ingredients; stir well, and pour over chicken. Cover and chill 8 hours. Remove chicken from refrigerator; let stand at room temperature 30 minutes. Cover and bake at 350° for 30 minutes. Uncover and drain liquid from baking dish, discarding liquid. Heat preserves in a small saucepan over low heat until warm. Brush over chicken. Bake, uncovered, 30 minutes more, basting occasionally with preserves. Sprinkle with pecans.

Grocery List: 8 boneless chicken breast halves, 12 oz. apricot nectar, 1 jar apricot preserves

Pantry Checklist: Allspice, Ginger, Salt, Pepper, Pecans

Hot Chicken Salad

1 cup cooked chicken breast, cubed
1 tsp. grated onion
½ cup sliced water chestnuts
1 cup bean sprouts, drained
1 tsp. lemon juice

1 cup chopped celery
½ tsp. salt
½ small jar pimientos
¾ cup mayonnaise
½ cup shredded sharp cheddar cheese

Mix all ingredients except cheese, and place in 9 x 13 baking dish. Sprinkle cheese on top and bake at 375° for 20 minutes.

   Delicious served with broccoli spears drizzled with melted lemon butter, and cranberry salad.

Grocery List: 1 whole chicken breast, 1 bunch celery, 1 small can water chestnuts, 1 jar pimientos, 1 can bean sprouts, 1 pkg. shredded sharp cheddar cheese

Pantry Checklist: Salt, Lemon juice, Onion, Mayonnaise

Chicken Supreme

4 chicken breasts, cooked and cubed
2 Tbsp. melted butter
2 hard-boiled eggs, diced finely
3 Tbsp. chopped parsley
Salt and pepper to taste
Parmesan cheese

1 cup sliced mushrooms
2 cups Sherry Wine Sauce
 (recipe below)
2 Tbsp. cooking wine
¼ tsp. tarragon

Cook and cube chicken breasts. Sauté mushrooms in butter. Add 1 cup wine sauce, chicken, hard-boiled eggs, parsley, cooking wine, and salt and pepper to taste. Add tarragon last; simmer 2 minutes. Spoon into crepes or toast cups; cover with remaining sauce and sprinkle with Parmesan cheese.

Sherry Wine Sauce:
2 Tbsp. butter
Salt and pepper to taste
Pinch of nutmeg

2 Tbsp. flour
1 egg yolk

2 cups milk
2 Tbsp. cooking sherry

Melt butter; add flour and stir with a whisk. Let foam and cook for 1 minute. Slowly add liquid, stirring constantly, until thickened. Add rest of ingredients.

Grocery List: 4 chicken breasts, 1 can sliced mushrooms or fresh mushrooms, 1 bunch fresh parsley, 1 bottle cooking sherry

Pantry Checklist: Butter, Eggs, Nutmeg, Salt, Pepper, Flour, Milk, Tarragon, Parmesan cheese

Kitchen Hint: Quantity of meat to buy per serving:
Boneless meat—¼ lb. per serving
Bone in—½ lb. per serving

Chicken Broccoli Casserole

4 large chicken breasts
2 cans cream of chicken soup
½ cup shredded cheddar cheese
⅛ tsp. curry powder

1 pkg. (10 oz.) frozen broccoli
1 cup mayonnaise
1 Tbsp. lemon juice
½ cup slivered almonds

Cook chicken until tender. Cool, bone, and cut into chunks. Cook broccoli according to directions and cool. Place chicken in bottom of 9 x 13 dish; put broccoli on top. Combine all other ingredients, except almonds, and pour on top. Bake at 350° for 1 hour. Sprinkle almonds on top.

rocery List: 4 large chicken breasts, 2 cans cream of chicken soup, 1 pkg. slivered almonds, 1 pkg. shredded cheddar cheese, 10 oz. pkg. frozen broccoli

Pantry Checklist: Lemon juice, Curry powder, Mayonnaise

Sesame Chicken

6 chicken breasts
1½ cups buttermilk
2 Tbsp. lemon juice

1 tsp. soy sauce
1 tsp. paprika
1 Tbsp. Italian seasoning

1 tsp. salt
1 tsp. pepper
2 cloves garlic, minced

4 cups soft bread crumbs
½ cup sesame seeds

¼ cup butter, melted

¼ cup melted shortening

Place chicken in dish with a tight lid. Combine next 8 ingredients and pour over chicken. Cover and refrigerate overnight. When ready to cook, drain, roll in bread crumbs, brush with mixture of shortening and butter, and sprinkle with sesame seeds. Bake at 350° for 45 minutes. Serve with rice and sweet-and-sour sauce.

Grocery List: 6 whole chicken breasts, 1 qt. buttermilk, 1 bottle Italian seasoning, Fresh garlic, 1 jar sesame seeds, Sweet-and-sour sauce, Rice

Pantry Checklist: Salt, Pepper, Butter, Paprika, Soy sauce, Lemon juice, Soft bread crumbs, Shortening

Bar-B-Q Chicken

2 fryers, cut up
3 Tbsp. brown sugar
¼ tsp. red pepper
  (optional)
¼ tsp. salt

1 large onion, chopped
¼ cup lemon Juice
3 Tbsp. Worcestershire
  sauce

3 Tbsp. vinegar
1 cup ketchup
1 Tbsp. prepared mustard
1¼ cups water

Salt and flour chicken; brown. Make a sauce of remaining ingredients. Boil sauce
and pour over chicken in greased large baking dish with liquid covering the
chicken. Cook at 350° for 1 hour (turn the pieces once). *Yield:* 6 to 8 servings.

Grocery List: 2 fryers (chicken)

Pantry Checklist: Onion, Vinegar, Brown sugar, Red pepper, Worcestershire sauce,
Mustard, Salt, Ketchup, Lemon juice

Chicken Cracker Casserole

5 to 6 chicken breasts
Bay leaf
Salt
2 sticks butter or margarine, melted
1 can cream of mushroom soup
1 small jar chopped pimientos

1 medium onion, chopped
Dash of lemon pepper
1 box Escort crackers
1 can cream of chicken soup
1 cup sour cream
1 can sliced water chestnuts

Boil chicken with onion, bay leaf, lemon pepper, and salt. Cool and cut into
chunks. Crumble 2 packages crackers in bottom of large glass casserole. Pour half
of melted butter over crackers. Mix other ingredients (except other 2 packages of
crackers and chicken). Spread chicken over crackers. Pour other ingredients over
chicken. Put remaining crumbs over this, then spoon remaining butter over all.
Bake at 350° for 30 minutes, until golden brown and bubbly.

Grocery List: 5 or 6 chicken breasts, 1 can cream of chicken soup, 1 can cream of
mushroom soup, 8 oz. sour cream, 1 jar pimientos, 1 can water
chestnuts, 1 box Escort crackers

Pantry Checklist: Margarine, Onion, Bay leaf, Lemon pepper, Salt

Chicken Rice Casserole

6 boneless, skinless chicken breasts
1 can French-style green beans, drained
1 Tbsp. pimiento, chopped
1 can cream of celery soup
½ cup mayonnaise
Soft buttered bread crumbs

1 box Uncle Ben's wild rice, cooked
1 can sliced water chestnuts, drained
¼ cup chopped onion
½ cup sour cream
Salt and pepper to taste

Cook chicken breasts, cool, and chop. Cook rice according to package directions. Mix chicken with all ingredients except buttered bread crumbs; place in greased 9 x 13 dish. Top with buttered bread crumbs. Bake at 350° for 30 minutes.

Grocery List: 6 chicken breast halves, 1 box Uncle Ben's Wild Rice, 1 can French-style green beans, 1 can cream of celery soup, 1 jar pimientos, 1 small can water chestnuts

Pantry Checklist: Onion, Sour cream, Mayonnaise, Bread crumbs, Salt and pepper

Crunchy Chicken Casserole

4 to 5 chicken breasts, cooked
   and chopped (reserve broth)
¾ cup chopped celery
½ cup reserved chicken broth
1½ cups Pepperidge Farm cornbread dressing mix (divided)

1 can cream of celery soup
¼ cup chopped onion
2 Tbsp. chopped pimientos
⅓ cup margarine, melted

Mix cooked chicken breasts with soup, onion, celery, pimientos, reserved broth, and ½ cup dressing mix. Place in casserole dish. Mix remaining dressing mix with butter and place on top of casserole. Bake at 350° for 30 minutes.

Grocery List: 4 to 5 chicken breasts, 1 can cream of celery soup, 1 bunch celery, 1 jar pimientos, 1 pkg. Pepperidge Farm cornbread dressing mix

Pantry Checklist: Margarine, Onion

Chicken Kiev

¼ cup softened butter
1 Tbsp. chopped parsley
1 Tbsp. finely cut chives
½ tsp. salt

⅛ tsp. pepper
1 Tbsp. minced onion
6 whole chicken breasts (boneless)
1 cup flour
2 eggs, beaten

Mix the first 6 ingredients and shape into 6 sticks; chill or freeze until firm. Wrap 6 whole boneless chicken breasts around butter sticks; secure with toothpicks. Roll in flour, dip in 2 beaten eggs, and roll in the following mixture:

1 pkg. dressing mix, crushed
1 cup Parmesan cheese

1 cup shredded cheddar cheese
1 Tbsp. parsley flakes

Place in shallow pan. Top each breast with 1 tablespoon butter. Bake at 350° for 1½ hours.

Grocery List: 6 whole chicken breasts, 1 bunch fresh parsley, 1 pkg. fresh or frozen chives, 1 pkg. Pepperidge Farm dressing mix, 1 pkg. shredded cheddar cheese, 1 jar Parmesan cheese

Pantry Checklist: Butter, Salt, Pepper, Onion, Eggs, Flour

Polynesian Chicken

1 cup pineapple juice
1 tsp. sugar

⅓ cup soy sauce
½ tsp. garlic powder

1 tsp. ginger
⅓ cup oil

6 chicken breasts

Pineapple slices

Combine first 6 ingredients and marinate chicken overnight. Cook on grill or on stovetop; top with pineapple slices. Baste with marinade.

Grocery List: 1 small can pineapple juice, 6 chicken breasts

Pantry Checklist: Soy sauce, Ginger, Sugar, Garlic powder, Oil

Chicken Spectacular

2 cups diced cooked chicken
2 cups cooked rice
1 can cream of celery soup
1 can (8 oz.) sliced water chestnuts
2 Tbsp. chopped onion
Buttered bread crumbs

1 pkg. (9 oz.) frozen baby green peas
½ cup mayonnaise
¼ tsp. salt
2 Tbsp. chopped pimiento
Pepper to taste
½ cup sliced almonds, toasted

Mix all ingredients except bread crumbs and almonds; place in 2-quart casserole. Cover with buttered bread crumbs and almonds and bake at 350° for 25 minutes.

Grocery List: 4 chicken breasts, 1 pkg. frozen baby peas, 1 can cream of celery soup, 1 can (8 oz.) sliced water chestnuts, 1 small jar pimientos, 1 small pkg. sliced almonds

Pantry Checklist: Mayonnaise, Rice, Salt, Pepper, Onion, Buttered bread crumbs

Kitchen Hint: Cooked rice freezes well. Cover and reheat in a microwave oven. Also, 1 cup of raw rice yields about 3 cups of cooked rice.

Chicken Shake and Bake

1 cup flour
1 cup cracker crumbs
1 tsp. oregano

2 tsp. salt
Paprika
1 tsp. basil

½ tsp. pepper
1 tsp. thyme
1 fryer or chicken pieces

Place first 8 ingredients in a plastic bag and mix well. Dip chicken in milk, then in crumbs. Bake or fry.

Grocery List: 1 pkg. cracker crumbs, 1 frying chicken

Pantry Checklist: Flour, Salt, Pepper, Paprika, Thyme, Oregano, Basil, Milk

Chicken Noodle Almond Casserole

4 large chicken breasts
½ soup can chicken broth
¼ green pepper, chopped
1 Tbsp. butter or margarine
8 green onion tops, sliced
1 pkg. (5 oz.) noodles,
  cooked and drained
Buttered bread crumbs

2 cans cream of chicken soup
4 to 5 stalks celery, chopped
¼ medium onion, chopped
1 can (4 oz.) mushrooms (with liquid)
3 Tbsp. cooking sherry
¼ to ½ cup slivered almonds
½ cup shredded cheddar cheese
Paprika

Cook chicken breasts; reserve broth. Cut chicken into cubes. Heat soup and broth; set aside. Sauté celery, green pepper, and onion in butter. Combine soup, cooked vegetables, mushrooms, onion tops, and cooking sherry.

Place a layer of cooked noodles, then a layer of chopped chicken, in a 2-quart casserole; cover with soup mixture and sprinkle with almonds. Repeat layers until all ingredients have been used. Cover top with cheese and buttered bread crumbs; sprinkle with paprika. Bake at 350° about 30 minutes, or until mixture bubbles. *Yield:* 8 servings.

Grocery List: 4 large chicken breasts, 2 cans cream of chicken soup, 1 bunch celery, 1 can (4 oz.) mushrooms, 1 pkg. (5 oz.) noodles, 1 pkg. almonds, 1 pkg. shredded cheddar cheese, Green onions, 1 green pepper

Pantry Checklist: Onion, Margarine, Cooking sherry, Bread crumbs, Paprika

Cranberry Chicken

1 small bottle Catalina dressing
1 can jellied cranberry sauce

1 pkg. dry onion soup mix
6 boneless chicken breasts

Mix Catalina dressing, onion soup mix, and cranberry sauce together with a wire whisk. Place chicken in greased baking dish; cover with the above mixture, and bake at 350° for 1½ hours. Serve over rice.

Grocery List: 6 chicken breasts, 1 small bottle Catalina dressing, 1 pkg. dry onion soup mix, 1 can jellied cranberry sauce

Note: This sauce makes enough for two meals; you can store the rest in the refrigerator.

Apricot Almond Chicken

1 bottle (8 oz.) Russian dressing
¾ cup apricot preserves
2 cups water
8 chicken breasts

1 pkg. onion soup mix
4 oz. slivered almonds
Butter

Mix Russian dressing, preserves, water, and soup mix; pour over chicken. Bake, uncovered, at 350° for 1½ hours. Baste 3 to 4 times with remaining mixture. Top with almonds sautéed in butter. Serve over rice. *Yield:* 10 servings.

Grocery List: 1 small bottle Russian dressing, 1 jar apricot preserves, 8 chicken breasts, 1 pkg. onion soup mix, 1 pkg. slivered almonds

Pantry Checklist: Butter

Kitchen Hint: When buying chicken, purchase enough for two meals. The above recipe can be made ahead and frozen. When needed, remove from freezer, thaw, and bake.

Chicken Dressing Casserole

6 chicken breasts, cooked and
    chopped into 1-inch pieces
    (reserve broth)
½ of (13 oz.) can evaporated milk
1 stick margarine

1 can cream of chicken soup
1 can cream of celery soup
2 cups chicken broth (1 can broth,
    1 cup from chicken)
1 pkg. cornbread stuffing mix

Place chicken in bottom of greased casserole dish. Mix soups and canned milk; pour over chicken. Mix broth and melted margarine with stuffing mix; spoon over chicken and soup mixture. Bake at 350° for 45 minutes.

Grocery List: 6 chicken breast halves, 1 can each cream of chicken and cream of celery soup, 13 oz. evaporated milk, 1 pkg. cornbread stuffing mix, 1 can chicken broth (use 1 cup broth from cooked chicken)

Pantry Checklist: Margarine

Ham Loaf

2 lbs. ham, ground
½ cup milk
¼ tsp. pepper

1 cup soft bread crumbs
2 eggs, beaten

Mix together and place in greased loaf pan. Top with the following sauce.

Sauce:
¼ cup vinegar
½ cup brown sugar

1 tsp. prepared mustard
¼ cup water

Mix together, pour on top of ham loaf, and bake at 350° for 1 hour.

Grocery List: 2 lbs. ham

Pantry Checklist: Soft bread crumbs, Milk, Eggs, Pepper, Vinegar, Prepared mustard, Brown sugar

Kitchen Hint: Save leftover ham; grind or chop in food processor and freeze to make ham loaf.

Cranberry Pork Roast or Pork Tenderloin

1 small bottle Catalina dressing
1 can jellied cranberry sauce

1 pkg. dry onion soup mix
1 large pork loin roast or pork tenderloin

Mix Catalina dressing, dry onion soup mix, and cranberry sauce together with a wire whisk. Place roast in large well-greased baking dish. Cover with the dressing and bake for 2 to 3 hours at 325° or until well done. (For tenderloin cook 45 minutes at 375°.) Serve with wild rice.

Grocery List: 1 large pork roast or pork tenderloin, 1 small bottle Catalina dressing, 1 pkg. dry onion soup mix, 1 can jellied cranberry sauce

Luau Ribs

2 jars (4½ oz.) strained peaches
  (baby food)
2 Tbsp. soy sauce
1 clove garlic, minced
1 tsp. salt
4 lbs. spareribs

½ cup ketchup
⅓ cup vinegar
½ cup brown sugar
2 tsp. ginger
Dash pepper

Mix all ingredients together except ribs. Cook ribs 1 hour in oven at 350°. Then cook on grill and baste often with above mixture.

Grocery List: 2 jars (4½ oz.) strained peaches (baby food section), 4 lbs. spareribs

Pantry Checklist: Ketchup, Vinegar, Soy sauce, Brown sugar, Garlic, Ginger, Salt, Pepper

Special Spaghetti Sauce

2 lb. ground chuck
1 large can (29 oz.) tomato sauce
2 tsp. chili powder
1 tsp. basil
1 tsp. garlic powder or fresh garlic
Dash cinnamon

1 large onion, chopped
1 can (12 oz.) tomato paste
1 tsp. pepper
2 Tbsp. brown sugar
1 Tbsp. vinegar
Salt to taste

Mix all ingredients in large bowl. Place in large pan and bake at 350° for 1 hour, stirring often. Serve over cooked pasta.

Grocery List: 2 lbs. ground chuck, 1 large can tomato sauce, 1 can (12 oz.) tomato paste

Pantry Checklist: Onion, Chili powder, Salt, Pepper, Brown sugar, Basil, Garlic, Vinegar, Cinnamon

Easy Spaghetti Sauce

1 jar spaghetti sauce
1 tsp. brown sugar
1 tsp. vinegar

1 lb. ground chuck
1 Tbsp. chili powder
1 clove garlic, minced

Mix the above ingredients together with mixer. Place in covered pan or dish and bake at 350° for 1 hour. Stir often. Serve over noodles.

Grocery List: 1 lb. ground chuck, 1 jar spaghetti sauce, Fresh garlic

Pantry Checklist: Brown sugar, Chili powder, Vinegar

Kitchen Hint: In all meat recipes containing cream soups, you can cut the fat by using light or nonfat soups. (You may have to increase salt to taste.)

Easy Oven Roast

1 roast, chuck or shoulder
1 can reduced-fat cream
   of chicken soup
Salt to taste

1 pkg. dry onion soup mix
1 tsp. Nature's Seasoning
1 to 2 Tbsp. Kitchen Bouquet

Place roast in roasting pan and half cover it with water. Bake at 350° for 1½ hours. Remove roast from pan and stir in soups and seasonings. Place roast back in mixture and bake for another two hours. Delicious! (makes its own gravy)

Grocery List: 1 roast, 1 pkg. dry onion soup mix, 1 can reduced-fat cream of chicken soup, 1 bottle Kitchen Bouquet (gravy section)

Pantry Checklist: Nature's Seasoning, Salt

Illustration: Susan Waters Sisson, 1993

Our home in Kenova, West Virginia—317 15th Street. The house was built in 1915.

Special Touring Events

In 1986 Michael was in the midst of *The Big Picture Tour*, which came to Huntington, West Virginia. They drove to our small town of Kenova and parked the bus near our house at 317 Fifteenth Street (now known as Michael W. Smith Drive). Many neighbors and sightseers wondered what was going on when they saw this bus, which took up half the block. Michael brought the whole band and crew (about twenty people, including Chris Harris and Chris Rodriguez), and we prepared dinner for them. Guys in the band still talk about this event with us. They enjoyed it so much that we gave them recipes for their wives. I served the following menu: Eye of Round Roast (page 145), Ham Loaf (page 140), Green Beans (page 116), Asparagus Casserole (page 121), Sweet Potato Casserole (page 118), Easy Tossed Salad (page 88), Cloverleaf Rolls (page 74), Cold Oven Pound Cake (page 168), Chocolate Cake with White Frosting (page 169), and Blackberry Cobbler (page 189).

Following dinner they went to an open field near our home and played football. The bus driver broke his leg and ended up in a cast; I'll bet he never forgets Kenova, West Virginia!

Then in November of 1989 Randy Travis came to Ohio to film a Red Cross disaster relief commercial. The setting was Proctorville, Ohio, in a field way out in the middle of nowhere. I have never done anything outside in such a barren place. It was cold and snowing; they wanted hot food, so we catered the event for about fifty people. (Obviously we used our coolers to keep the food and beverages hot. We had heated stones in the bottom and large thermos containers of hot drinks.) We set up picnic tables to serve on.

My menu for that event was: Vegetable Soup (page 106), Green Beans (page 116), Potatoes au Gratin (page 116), Chicken Shake and Bake (page 137), Cloverleaf Rolls (page 74), Hot Spiced Apple Cider (page 37), Coffee and Tea, Cold Oven Pound Cake (page 168), Apple Crisp (page 188), and Texas Chocolate Cake (page 171).

Baked Steak

6 pieces cubed steak
1 can low-fat cream of chicken soup
Salt and pepper to taste

3 Tbsp. dry onion soup mix
1 to 2 Tbsp. Kitchen Bouquet
¾ cup water

Flour and brown meat in small amount of oil. Season with salt and pepper. Remove steak to a greased casserole dish. Mix 2 to 3 Tbsp. flour with remaining drippings in pan and mix well. Add onion soup mix, chicken soup, Kitchen Bouquet, water, and salt and pepper to taste. Pour over steak and bake at 350° for 2½ hours.

Grocery List: 6 pieces cubed steak, 1 pkg. dry onion soup mix, 1 can low-fat cream of chicken soup, 1 bottle Kitchen Bouquet (gravy section)

Pantry Checklist: Salt, Pepper

Pepper Steak

1½ lbs. top round steak (cut into cubes)
2 Tbsp. olive oil
2 cups boiling water
2 Tbsp. cornstarch
1 to 2 Tbsp. Kitchen Bouquet
1 large onion, quartered

2 cloves garlic, minced
2 beef bouillon cubes
2 Tbsp. soy sauce
½ cup water
1 green pepper, cut into chunks
Salt and pepper to taste

Brown steak and garlic in olive oil; then mix bouillon cubes with boiling water and mix well. Pour over beef with soy sauce and cook until tender (about 20 minutes). Mix cornstarch with ½ cup water and mix in with beef to thicken; then add Kitchen Bouquet. Add peppers and onions; cook until crisp-tender. Season with salt and pepper. Serve over rice.

Grocery List: 1½ lbs. round steak, Fresh garlic, 1 green pepper, 1 bottle Kitchen Bouquet (gravy section)

Pantry Checklist: Bouillon cubes, Cornstarch, Soy sauce, Onion, Olive oil, Salt, Pepper

Eye of Round Roast

1 eye of round roast
1 pkg. dry onion soup mix
Salt to taste

1 can cream of chicken soup
1 to 2 Tbsp. Kitchen Bouquet

Place roast in foil large enough to seal well. Cover roast with soups and seasonings. Seal well in foil. Place in baking dish. Bake at 350° for 2 hours. Reduce temperature to 325° and cook for another 1½ hours.

 Grocery List: Eye of round roast, 1 can cream of chicken soup, 1 pkg. dry onion soup mix, 1 bottle Kitchen Bouquet

Pantry Checklist: Salt

Beef Tenderloin

1 whole beef tenderloin

Marinade:
1 cup pineapple juice
1 tsp. ginger
½ tsp. garlic powder

⅓ cup soy sauce
1 tsp. sugar
⅓ cup oil

Mix marinade ingredients. Marinate the tenderloin overnight in refrigerator. Bring the roast to room temperature; drain and bake, uncovered, at 400° for 45 to 60 minutes, depending on how well done you like beef.

Mushroom Sauce:
1 pkg. mushroom gravy mix
Dash of garlic salt
Drippings from meat

1 pkg. brown gravy mix
2 Tbsp. Worcestershire sauce

Mix as per gravy directions; add other ingredients and serve over meat.

Grocery List: 1 whole beef tenderloin, 1 pkg. mushroom gravy mix, 1 pkg. brown gravy mix

Pantry Checklist: Soy sauce, Ginger, Sugar, Garlic powder, Oil, Worcestershire sauce, Garlic salt

Lasagna

1 lb. ground chuck
⅓ lb. sausage
Garlic salt to taste
1 Tbsp. Italian seasoning
¼ tsp. oregano
2 Tbsp. parsley flakes
1½ tsp. salt
2 tsp. sugar
2 cans (16 oz. each) tomatoes

2 cans (6 oz. each) tomato paste
1 large onion, chopped
1 tsp. salt
2 Tbsp. vegetable oil
1 lb. lasagna noodles
3 cups cottage cheese
1 lb. mozzarella cheese, grated
½ cup grated Parmesan cheese

Brown ground chuck and sausage in a large skillet. Remove from heat and place in large saucepan. Add next 9 ingredients and simmer for 30 minutes. Add salt and vegetable oil to 4 quarts of rapidly boiling water; add noodles and cook 10 minutes, or until tender. Drain; rinse in cold water and rinse again. Layer the sauce, noodles, cottage cheese, mozzarella cheese, and Parmesan cheese in a large casserole until all ingredients are used, ending with Parmesan cheese. Bake at 375° for 30 minutes.

Grocery List: 1 lb. ground chuck, 1 lb. sausage, 2 16-oz. cans tomatoes, 2 6-oz. cans tomato paste, 1 large cottage cheese, 1 jar Parmesan cheese, 1 lb. mozzarella cheese, 1 lb. lasagna noodles

Pantry Checklist: Garlic salt, Italian seasoning, Oregano, Parsley flakes, Sugar, Salt, Onion, Oil

Meat Loaf

2 lbs. ground chuck
2 eggs, lightly beaten
½ green pepper, chopped
Salt and pepper to taste
1 can Hunt's special tomato sauce

1 onion, chopped
18 Ritz crackers, crushed
½ cup ketchup
½ cup brown sugar

Mix all ingredients (except ketchup and brown sugar) together and place in greased loaf pan. Mix ketchup and brown sugar; spread on top. Bake at 350° for 2 hours.

Grocery List: 2 lbs. ground chuck, 1 green pepper, 1 can Hunt's special tomato sauce, 1 box Ritz crackers

Pantry Checklist: Onion, Salt, Pepper, Brown sugar, Ketchup, Eggs

Vegetarian Burritos

½ cup sliced onions
1 cup mushrooms, sliced
½ tsp. salt
1 cup packed fresh spinach
   leaves, chopped
½ cup shredded Monterey
   Jack or mozzarella cheese
12 flour tortillas (8-inch)

2 Tbsp. oil
1 can artichoke hearts, drained
   and chopped
1 small can chopped
   green chilies, drained
½ cup shredded cheddar cheese
¼ tsp. each basil, cumin, and pepper

Sauté onions in oil for 2 to 3 minutes. Add mushrooms. Sauté 1 minute. Remove from heat; add remaining ingredients (except cheese and tortillas). Toss until blended. Fill 12 8-inch flour tortillas; top with cheese, roll up, and place in greased baking pan. Bake at 350° for 15 to 20 minutes. Serve with salsa, sour cream, and guacamole.

Grocery List: 1 pkg. fresh mushrooms, 1 can artichoke hearts, 1 pkg. each cheddar and mozzarella cheese, 1 pkg. fresh spinach, 1 pkg. 8-inch flour tortillas, 1 small can green chilies, Salsa, Sour cream

Pantry Checklist: Onions, Oil, Salt, Basil, Pepper

Chicken Chimichangas

½ cup picante sauce or salsa
3 cups cooked, chopped chicken
½ small onion, diced
1 tsp. ground cumin
1 tsp. dried oregano

½ tsp. salt
1 tsp. cilantro
10 flour tortillas (8-inch)
1½ cups shredded cheddar cheese

Combine first 7 ingredients in Dutch oven; cook over medium-low heat, until most liquid evaporates. Spoon ⅓ cup mixture into center of tortilla; top with cheese. Fold in 2 sides of tortilla to enclose filling, then fold over top and bottom edges and secure with toothpicks. Place folded side down on greased baking sheets. Coat with cooking spray. Bake at 425° for 8 minutes. Turn; bake 5 more minutes. Remove picks. Serve with salsa, sour cream, or guacamole.

Grocery List: 1 jar picante sauce or salsa, 4 chicken breasts, 1 pkg. 8-inch flour tortillas, 1 pkg. shredded cheddar cheese, Sour cream, Guacamole, Cilantro

Pantry Checklist: Onion, Cumin, Oregano, Salt

Jalapeño Chicken

1 small can green chilies, chopped
1 garlic clove, chopped

1 medium onion, chopped
2 Tbsp. oil

Cook the above together until tender.

Add to the above:
1 can cream of mushroom soup
1 pkg. (10 oz.) frozen chopped spinach,
  cooked in microwave and drained
2 cups Monterey Jack cheese, shredded

½ tsp. salt
1 pt. sour cream
4 chicken breasts, cooked and chopped

Alternate layers of tortilla chips, chicken mixture, and Monterey Jack cheese. Bake at 350° for 30 minutes.

Grocery List: 1 small can green chilies, 1 can cream of mushroom soup, Fresh garlic, 10 oz. pkg. frozen chopped spinach, 1 pt. sour cream, 4 chicken breasts, 1 bag tortilla chips, 1 pkg. Monterey Jack cheese

Pantry Checklist: Onion, Oil, Salt

Beef and Salsa Burritos

1¼ lbs. ground chuck
½ tsp. ground cumin
1 pkg. (10 oz.) frozen chopped
  spinach, thawed and well drained
8 medium flour tortillas, warmed

1½ Tbsp. chili powder
Salt and pepper to taste
1¼ cups salsa
1 cup shredded cheddar cheese

In large nonstick skillet, cook ground chuck until well done. Pour off drippings. Season beef with chili powder, cumin, salt, and pepper. Stir in spinach and salsa and heat through. Remove from heat and stir in cheese. Spoon ½ cup mixture into center of each tortilla. Fold bottom edge up over filling; fold sides to center, overlapping edges. Serve with sour cream and guacamole.

Grocery List: 1¼ lbs. ground chuck, 10 oz. frozen chopped spinach, 1 jar salsa, 1 pkg. shredded cheddar cheese, 1 pkg. flour tortillas, Sour cream, Guacamole

Pantry Checklist: Chili powder, Cumin, Salt, Pepper

Taco Pie

1 lb. ground chuck
1 pkg. taco seasoning mix
1¼ cups milk
3 eggs
1 cup shredded Monterey Jack or cheddar cheese
½ cup chopped onion
1 can chopped green chilies, drained
¾ cup Bisquick baking mix
2 tomatoes, sliced

Cook ground chuck and onion until well done; drain. Stir in taco seasoning and spread in 10-inch greased pie plate. Sprinkle with chilies. Mix milk, Bisquick, and eggs until well blended; pour over other mixture. Bake at 400° for 25 minutes. Remove from oven. Top with tomatoes and cheese; bake for 8 for 10 minutes or until well done. Serve with sour cream and shredded lettuce.

Grocery List:

1 lb. ground chuck, 1 pkg. taco seasoning mix, 1 small can chopped green chilies, 1 small box Bisquick, 2 tomatoes, 1 pkg. shredded cheddar cheese, 1 head lettuce, Sour cream

Pantry Checklist:

Onion, Milk, Eggs

White Chili

1 lb. cooked, chopped
   chicken breasts (reserve broth)
1 can chicken broth
1 small can chopped green chilies
½ tsp. cayenne pepper
Salt to taste
½ cup onion, chopped
2 cloves garlic, chopped
2 cans (16 oz. each) white beans, drained
½ tsp. oregano
⅛ tsp. cloves
2 Tbsp. cornstarch

Save broth from chicken; add canned chicken broth and enough water to broth from chicken to make 5 cups of liquid. In large pan combine liquid, chicken, beans, chilies, oregano, cayenne pepper, cloves, salt, and cornstarch (mixed with ¼ cup water). Cook 30 minutes at medium heat; reduce to low heat and cook another 20 minutes.

*Grocery List:*

1 lb. chicken breasts, 2 16-oz. cans white beans, 1 can chicken broth, 1 small can chopped green chilies, Fresh garlic

Pantry Checklist:

Onion, Oregano, Cayenne pepper, Cloves, Cornstarch, Salt

Mexican Ranch Chicken

4 boneless chicken breasts
¼ tsp. pepper
1 green pepper, chopped
2 cans (10 oz. each) diced tomatoes
   with green chilies, undrained
12 corn tortillas (6-inch), cut into quarters
2 cups shredded cheddar cheese

¼ tsp. salt
2 Tbsp. butter
1 medium onion, chopped
1 can cream of mushroom soup
1 can cream of chicken soup

Cook chicken with salt and pepper until done; chop and set aside. Melt butter in large skillet over medium heat; add green pepper and onion and stir-fry until crisp-tender. Remove from heat. Stir in chicken, tomatoes, mushroom soup, and chicken soup.

Place ⅓ of tortillas in bottom of lightly greased 9 x 13 baking dish; top with ⅓ of chicken mixture and sprinkle with ⅔ cup cheese. Repeat layers, reserving last ⅔ cup cheese. Bake at 325° for 35 minutes; sprinkle with reserved cheese and bake 5 additional minutes. Let stand 5 minutes before serving.

Grocery List: 4 boneless chicken breasts, 1 green pepper, 2 10-oz. cans tomatoes with chilies, 1 can each mushroom soup and chicken soup, 1 pkg. corn tortillas, 1 pkg. shredded cheddar cheese

Pantry Checklist: Salt, Pepper, Butter, Onion

Three-Pepper Quesadillas

1 cup green pepper, thinly sliced
1 cup yellow pepper, thinly sliced
1 cup red pepper, thinly sliced
1 pkg. fresh mushrooms, sliced

1 cup onion, thinly sliced
2 cups shredded cheddar cheese
¼ cup margarine
1 pkg. flour tortillas (8 inch)

Sauté peppers, mushrooms, and onions in margarine in a large skillet. Set aside. Spread a layer of cheese, peppers, and then another layer of cheese; fold over and brown in skillet on medium heat until cheese melts. Slice and serve with shredded lettuce, salsa, and sour cream.

Grocery List: 1 green pepper, 1 yellow pepper, 1 red pepper, 1 pkg. mushrooms, 1 large pkg. shredded cheddar cheese, 1 pkg. flour tortillas, Lettuce, Salsa, Sour cream

Pantry Checklist: Margarine, Onion

Ryan and Whitney, his waitress at the café, decide upon the menu.

Ryan's Café

Michael's oldest child, Ryan, has learned to cook from his mom and me. He enjoys cooking so much that he often cooks for the family.

"Mom, I'll do lunch," he may say. Or he will plan to do lunch for Whitney and her friend Megen. He looks in the refrigerator to see what he can use; then he plans the menu.

Several times he has had a little café. One time the kids were home for a snow day, and they were bored. So Ryan set up tables in the great room, planned his menu, and then invited the neighbors over. He fixed a big lunch for everybody and charged a dollar for the meal. He boiled noodles and made Quesadillas (page 152) and sandwiches. That time he even wrote out the menu and placed it on the tables so everyone could order.

All the invited guests had to sit there as if it were a real restaurant. He even had a staff. His sister Whitney waited tables with her friend Megen. They wore aprons and took orders.

My grandchildren have always liked playing restaurant. One Christmas Debbie and Michael gave them a set that included a menu board for "specials of the day," order forms you could fill out for your selection, bills, and a cash register—everything you needed to play restaurant.

The food at Ryan's Café is always good, but Debbie says that the kitchen is frequently a disaster. Every dish and pan is dirty, because Ryan doesn't like to clean up. Still, Debbie will endure the mess for his cooking events.

Ryan's Orange Julep

1 can (6 oz.) frozen orange juice   1 cup water
1 cup milk   ½ cup sugar
1 tsp. vanilla   1½ cups shaved ice

Combine all ingredients with electric blender; blend until smooth. Serve immediately.

Grocery List: 1 can (6 oz.) frozen orange juice

Pantry Checklist: Vanilla, Milk, Sugar

Ryan's Quesadillas

1 pkg. flour tortillas   Velveeta cheese, sliced

Spray skillet with cooking spray; place Velveeta cheese on flour tortillas, fold in half, and cook over medium heat until cheese melts. Slice and serve.

Grocery List: 1 pkg. flour tortillas, 1 pkg. Velveeta cheese, Cooking spray

Ryan's Pizza

12-inch pizza crust   1 jar Pizza Quick sauce
Shredded American cheese

For a full-size pizza, spoon ½ jar of Pizza Quick sauce on a 12-inch pizza crust. Top with cheese and bake at 400° until cheese melts (about 8 to 10 minutes).

Desserts

Whitney (Michael's oldest daughter), Mimi (that's what the grandkids call me),
and Megen Sharp make sugar cookies for Christmas.

M ICHAEL'S FAVORITE CAKES ARE CHOCOLATE Cake with White Frosting (page 169) and Cheesecake (page 181). (Paul says that Michael changed from white cake to chocolate as he grew older because chocolate was Paul's favorite.)

Michael is also an M & M lover. In fact, when he is on tour, the snacks and meals are catered because it's too difficult to go out and eat and still be back in time for sound check. So Michael always snacks in his dressing room. I think Amy Grant told the caterers that Michael loved M & M's, so for a while everywhere he went there was an extra-large bowl in his dressing room. (He is kind of like his dad; if something is chocolate, it can't be all bad.) After a couple of years he asked that they cut back a little.

A friend of ours also went to one of his concerts and wanted to do something for him. She took him a cookie jar full of M & M's. He likes them cold. There is always a sack of M & M's in the freezer at his studio in Franklin.

One of the grandchildren's favorite things to do with me is bake cookies. They love sugar cookies, for which I use my mom's recipe (page 185). We get out every cookie cutter I have, and they choose the cutter according to the holiday. We make a sugar glaze (which they love), and Whitney, Anna, Emily, Mary Claire, and Caroline sprinkle red and green sugar crystals, M & M's, or anything they can find on the cookies. For Halloween, we use orange, black, and white sugars. For Valentine's Day we use heart-shaped cookie cutters. For every three cookies we decorate, two go into their mouths! My kitchen is a sea of sugar and five colored mouths! Ryan and Tyler don't make the cookies—they just eat them.

We also have had many tea parties. We have poured more tea in and out of cups than you can imagine, since the fun is in the pouring of the tea. We serve everything from saltine crackers to cookies and cake. Many of these tea parties occur outside. The girls bring their teddy bears as guests.

To me, dessert is the perfect ending to a good meal. There are many ways to be creative with desserts; I hope you will try many of the ones in this section. Some of my neighbors enjoyed the tasting parties in preparation for this book!

Easy Flaky Pastry

1½ cups flour
1 stick margarine

1 tsp. salt
5 Tbsp. ice water

Place flour, salt, and margarine in the food processor and mix just until margarine is in small pieces, then add ice water and pulse off and on until dough forms a ball. It is best to run the processor off and on, rather than constantly, during this process. Place dough in refrigerator until it is chilled. Roll out dough and place in 2 pie pans.

Pantry Checklist: Flour, Margarine, Salt

Kitchen Hint: Store baking soda, flour, salt, sugar, flour, seasonings, and flavorings in a cabinet close to your mixer.

Hot Water Pie Crust

¾ cup shortening
¼ cup boiling water
1 tsp. salt

1 Tbsp. milk
2 cups flour

Place shortening in mixing bowl. Add milk and boiling water. With fork or wire whisk, mix until smooth and thick. Add flour and salt; stir until dough forms. Shape into two smooth balls; wrap in waxed paper and refrigerate overnight. When ready to use, remove from refrigerator and allow to reach room temperature (about 15 minutes). Roll out dough and place in 2 pie pans.

Grocery List: 1 small can shortening

Pantry Checklist: Flour, Salt, Milk

Key Lime Pie

1 envelope unflavored gelatin
4 eggs, separated
⅓ cup lime juice
2 tsp. grated lime rind
1 baked pie shell

¼ cup cold water
1 cup sugar, divided
½ tsp. salt
Green food coloring

Bake pie shell according to package directions. Soften gelatin in cold water. Beat egg yolks; add ½ cup sugar, lime juice, and salt. Cook egg mixture in double boiler, stirring constantly until thickened. Add grated rind and gelatin; stir until gelatin is dissolved. Tint pale green with food coloring. Cool. Beat egg whites until stiff but not dry; add remaining sugar slowly, beating after each addition and fold into lime mixture. Pour into baked 9-inch pie shell. Chill until firm.

Grocery List: 1 pkg. unflavored gelatin, 1 pie shell, 2 limes

Pantry Checklist: Sugar, Eggs, Salt, Green food coloring

Chocolate Mousse Pie

4 squares semisweet baking chocolate
1 pkg. (3 oz.) cream cheese
1 carton (8 oz.) frozen
   whipped topping

⅓ cup milk
2 Tbsp. sugar
1 chocolate graham
   cracker crust (9-inch)

Melt chocolate and 2 tablespoons of the milk. Beat in cream cheese, sugar, and remaining milk until smooth. Refrigerate 10 minutes. Fold in whipped topping and mix until smooth. Pour into pie crust and freeze. Garnish with extra whipped topping and grated chocolate.

Grocery List: 1 pkg. semisweet baking chocolate, 3 oz. cream cheese, 8 oz. whipped topping, 1 chocolate graham cracker crust

Pantry Checklist: Milk, Sugar

Desserts

Pecan Pie

½ cup butter, melted
½ cup white sugar
4 eggs, lightly beaten
1 tsp. vanilla
1 unbaked pie shell

½ cup firmly packed brown sugar
1 Tbsp. flour
1 cup light corn syrup
1½ cups chopped pecans

Beat butter at medium speed with an electric mixer until creamy. Add brown and white sugars and flour, beating well. Add eggs, 1 at a time, beating after each addition. Add corn syrup and vanilla, beating until well blended. Stir in chopped pecans and pour in unbaked pie shell. Bake at 325° for 50 minutes or until set.

Grocery List: 1 lb. butter, 1 small pkg. pecans, 1 bottle light corn syrup, 1 pie shell (in frozen foods section)

Pantry Checklist: Brown and white sugar, Flour, Eggs, Vanilla

Lemon Pie

1¼ cups sugar
¼ tsp. salt
4 large egg yolks
4 Tbsp. butter, softened
1 baked pie shell

½ cup cornstarch
2 cups water
½ cup fresh lemon juice
2 tsp. grated lemon rind

Bake pie shell according to package directions. Combine sugar, cornstarch, and salt; mix well. Gradually stir in the water until mixture is blended and smooth. Heat to boiling over medium heat, stirring constantly for 1 minute. Remove from heat. In small bowl, whisk egg yolks until blended. Pour in about ½ cup hot mixture, whisking until blended. Stir in lemon juice, butter, and lemon rind. Mix and pour into cornstarch mixture in pan. Stir until blended. Heat until mixture is thickened. Pour into completely cooled pastry shell. Refrigerate until served. Top with whipped topping.

Grocery List: 3 lemons, 1 pie shell, Whipped topping

Pantry Checklist: Sugar, Cornstarch, Butter, Salt, Eggs

Desserts

Chocolate Chess Pie

1½ cups sugar
3½ Tbsp. cocoa
1 tsp. vanilla
1 small can (¾ cup) evaporated milk
1 unbaked pie shell

1 stick butter
⅛ tsp. salt
2 eggs
2 Tbsp. flour

Mix sugar, cocoa, flour, and butter. Cream well and add eggs; beat with mixer for 2 minutes. Add salt, milk, and vanilla. Pour filling into unbaked pie shell and bake at 400° for 10 minutes. Reduce temperature to 325° and bake for another 35 to 45 minutes until set. Serve with whipped topping and grated chocolate. Very rich!

Grocery List: 1 can evaporated milk, 1 box cocoa, 1 pie shell, Whipped topping, 1 box semisweet baking chocolate

Pantry Checklist: Sugar, Butter, Eggs, Salt, Vanilla, Flour

Coconut Cream Pie

1 cup sugar
Dash of salt
3 egg yolks
1 tsp. vanilla
1 baked pie shell

4½ Tbsp. cornstarch
2¼ cups milk
2 Tbsp. butter
¾ cup coconut

Bake pie shell according to package directions. Mix sugar, cornstarch, and salt. Add milk and mix well. Cook over medium heat until it begins to thicken. Meanwhile, beat egg yolks, then add ½ cup of hot mixture to egg mixture. Then add egg mixture to the remaining custard. Cook until thick. Remove from heat. Add butter, vanilla, and coconut and let cool. Place in baked pie shell and chill. When ready to serve, top with whipped topping.

Grocery List: 1 qt. milk, 1 pkg. coconut, 1 pie shell, Whipped topping

Pantry Checklist: Sugar, Cornstarch, Butter, Eggs, Salt, Vanilla

Butterscotch Cream Pie

1 cup brown sugar
Dash of salt
3 egg yolks, beaten
2 Tbsp. butter

4 Tbsp. cornstarch
2¼ cups milk
1 tsp. vanilla
1 baked pie shell

Bake pie shell according to package directions. Mix sugar, cornstarch, and salt in saucepan; add milk. Cook over medium heat, stirring constantly with wire whisk. When mixture begins to thicken, add a little of the hot mixture to the egg yolks; mix well and add egg mixture to custard. Continue cooking until mixture is thickened. Remove from heat and add butter and vanilla. Pour into baked pie crust and chill. Top with whipped topping.

Grocery List: 1 box brown sugar, 1 qt. milk, Whipped topping, 1 pie shell

Pantry Checklist: Cornstarch, Butter, Salt, Vanilla, Eggs

Kitchen Hint: Before measuring corn syrup or honey, oil the cup with cooking oil and rinse in hot water.

Chocolate Pecan Pie

1 cup sugar
3 eggs, slightly beaten
¼ tsp. salt
½ cup chopped pecans
1 unbaked pie shell

¼ cup butter, melted
¾ cup light corn syrup
1 tsp. vanilla
½ cup chocolate chips

Cream sugar and butter. Add eggs, corn syrup, salt, and vanilla. Mix until blended. Spread pecans and chocolate chips in bottom of pie shell. Pour filling into shell. Bake at 375° for 40 to 50 minutes.

Grocery List: 1 bottle light corn syrup, 1 pkg. pecans, 1 small pkg. chocolate chips, 1 pie shell

Pantry Checklist: Butter, Sugar, Salt, Vanilla, Eggs

Pumpkin Pie

1¾ cups sugar
2 tsp. cinnamon
½ tsp. cloves
1 can (29 oz.) pumpkin
2 unbaked pie shells

1 tsp. salt
1 tsp. ginger
4 eggs, lightly beaten
2 cans (12 oz. each) evaporated milk

Combine sugar, salt, cinnamon, ginger, and cloves in bowl and set aside. Beat eggs lightly and stir in pumpkin; add to sugar-spice mixture. Gradually stir in evaporated milk. Pour into pie shells and bake at 425° for 15 minutes. Reduce heat to 350° and continue baking for 35 to 40 minutes.

Grocery List: 2 cans evaporated milk, 2 pie shells, 1 can (29 oz.) pumpkin

Pantry Checklist: Salt, Cinnamon, Ginger, Cloves, Eggs, Sugar

Graham Cracker Pie

1 cup sugar
Dash of salt
3 egg yolks, beaten
2 Tbsp. butter

4½ Tbsp. cornstarch
2 cups milk
1 tsp. vanilla
1 graham cracker crust

Mix sugar, cornstarch, and salt. Add milk and cook over medium heat until mixture begins to thicken. Remove from heat and mix ½ cup mixture with the egg yolks. Return egg mixture to pan and continue to cook until thickened. Remove from heat and add vanilla and butter. Place in graham cracker crust and chill. Top with whipped topping and 2 to 3 tablespoons graham cracker crumbs.

Grocery List: 2 graham cracker crusts, 1 qt. milk, Whipped topping

Pantry Checklist: Vanilla, Butter, Eggs, Salt, Sugar, Cornstarch

Note: A 13¾-ounce box of graham crackers, finely crushed, will make three 9-inch pie crusts.

Strawberry Heaven Pie

6 egg whites (at room temperature)
2 cups sugar
2 tsp. lemon juice
12 oz. whipped topping

⅛ tsp. salt
2 tsp. vanilla
Fresh strawberries

Beat egg whites and salt until stiff, but not dry. Gradually add 1 cup sugar, beating well after each addition. Add vanilla and second cup of sugar, alternating with lemon juice; beat until all sugar is dissolved and the meringue is stiff, approximately 15 minutes. Place the meringue into a well-greased and floured (rim too) 10-inch pie plate. Pile the meringue so it is higher in the middle and slants down to outside of pie plate. Bake at 275° for 1½ hours. Increase the heat to 300° and bake 30 minutes longer. The meringue will puff up while it is baking, then crack and fall in the middle as it cools. When cool, fill with whipped topping and sliced fresh strawberries that have been sweetened. When filling, start with whipped topping, then berries. Top layer will be whipped topping. Decorate with whole berries and chill before serving. When finished, you will have 3 layers of whipped topping and 2 layers of strawberries.

Grocery List: 1 dozen eggs, 1 qt. fresh strawberries, 12 oz. whipped topping

Pantry Checklist: Salt, Vanilla, Lemon juice, Sugar

French Coconut Pie

3 eggs, lightly beaten
1 tsp. vanilla
1 cup flaked coconut

1½ cups sugar
½ cup melted butter
1 unbaked pie shell

Mix first 5 ingredients and pour into pie shell. Bake at 400° for 15 minutes. Reduce heat to 350° and continue baking for 20 to 45 minutes.

Grocery List: 1 pkg. coconut, 1 pie shell

Pantry Checklist: Sugar, Eggs, Vanilla, Butter

Nan's Angel Pie

Crust:

⅛ tsp. salt
½ tsp. vanilla
1 cup sugar

½ tsp. cream of tartar
4 egg whites (at room temperature)

Add salt, cream of tartar, and vanilla to egg whites; beat until whites begin to hold shape. Add sugar gradually and beat until very stiff. Pour into a 10-inch buttered pie plate. Bake at 250° for 1½ hours. Cool.

Filling:

4 egg yolks, beaten
1 Tbsp. lemon peel, grated
2 Tbsp. lemon juice

½ cup sugar
⅛ tsp. salt
¼ cup crushed pineapple in syrup

Beat yolks slightly; add sugar, lemon peel, salt, lemon juice, and pineapple. Cook until thick. If filling is too thick, add small amount of hot water. Cool and pour into meringue crust.

Topping:

½ pt. whipping cream   2 Tbsp. sugar   ½ tsp. vanilla

Whip cream and add remaining ingredients. Spread over filling. Chill overnight before serving.

Grocery List: 1 pt. whipping cream, 1 small can crushed pineapple, 1 lemon

Pantry Checklist: Cream of tartar, Vanilla, Sugar, Salt, Eggs

Chocolate Mint Pie

½ gallon pink peppermint ice cream   ½ gallon green peppermint ice cream
2 chocolate crumb pie shells (9-inch)

Scoop alternately pink and green ice cream into each pie shell; freeze overnight. Cut into wedges and serve with Hot Fudge Sauce (page 183).

Grocery List: ½ gallon pink peppermint ice cream, ½ gallon green peppermint ice cream, 2 chocolate crumb pie shells (9-inch)

Peanut Butter Pie

1 pkg. (8 oz.) cream cheese
2 cups powdered sugar
2 cartons (8 oz. each) frozen
   whipped topping
Chocolate syrup

1 cup milk
⅔ cup crunchy peanut butter
2 chocolate crumb pie shells
Peanuts

Mix cream cheese, milk, sugar, and peanut butter. Add whipped topping. Pour into pie shells. Garnish with peanuts and chocolate syrup. Cover and freeze.

Grocery List: 8 oz. cream cheese, 1 box powdered sugar, 2 cartons (8 oz. each) whipped topping, 2 chocolate crumb pie shells, 1 can chocolate syrup, 1 can peanuts

Pantry Checklist: Milk, Crunchy peanut butter

Cherry Pie

1 cup sugar
¼ tsp. salt
¼ tsp. red food coloring
⅛ tsp. almond flavoring
2 unbaked pie shells

3 Tbsp. cornstarch
1 cup cherry juice
2 cans (16 oz. each) red tart pitted
   cherries, drained (reserve juice)

Mix sugar, cornstarch, and salt in a saucepan. Add cherry juice and food coloring; stir until smooth. Cook until thickened and clear, stirring constantly. Add cherries and almond flavoring. Pour into unbaked crust and top with the other crust. Bake at 375° for 30 minutes or until brown.

Grocery List: 2 cans red tart pitted cherries, 2 pie crusts

Pantry Checklist: Sugar, Cornstarch, Salt, Red food coloring, Almond flavoring

Chocolate Cream Pie

1 cup sugar
¼ cup cocoa
2¼ cups milk
⅛ tsp. almond flavoring
2 Tbsp. butter

4½ Tbsp. cornstarch
Dash of salt
3 egg yolks, beaten
½ tsp. vanilla flavoring
1 baked pie shell

Bake pie shell according to package directions. Mix sugar, cornstarch, cocoa, and salt. Blend in milk and cook on medium heat until mixture begins to thicken. Remove from heat and mix ½ cup mixture with the beaten egg yolks. Return egg mixture to pan and continue to cook until thickened. Remove from heat; add flavorings and 2 tablespoons of butter. Pour in cooled pie crust and top with whipped topping.

Grocery List: 1 qt. milk, 1 pie shell, Whipped topping

Pantry Checklist: Sugar, Cornstarch, Salt, Eggs, Almond extract, Cocoa, Vanilla, Butter

Fudge Pie

½ cup margarine
2 squares semisweet baking
   chocolate, melted
¼ cup flour
1 tsp. vanilla

1 unbaked pie shell
1 cup sugar
Pinch of salt
2 eggs, beaten
½ cup chopped pecans

Cream margarine and sugar. Add chocolate, salt, flour, eggs, and vanilla; blend thoroughly. Fold in nuts. Pour filling into pie shell; bake at 325° for 30 minutes. Serve with whipped topping.

Grocery List: 1 pie shell, 1 box semisweet baking chocolate, 1 pkg. pecans, Whipped topping

Pantry Checklist: Margarine, Sugar, Salt, Flour, Vanilla, Eggs

Fresh Peach Pie

3 Tbsp. dry peach gelatin
3 Tbsp. cornstarch
1 cup water

1 cup sugar
5 fresh peaches, sliced
1 baked pie shell

Bake pie shell according to package directions. Cook first 4 ingredients until thickened. Add peaches and pour filling into baked pie shell. Garnish with whipped topping.

Grocery List: 1 pkg. peach gelatin, 5 fresh peaches, 1 pie shell, Whipped topping

Pantry Checklist: Sugar, Cornstarch

Cranberry-Orange Cake

2½ cups all-purpose flour, sifted
1 cup sugar
1 tsp. salt
1 tsp. baking soda
1 tsp. baking powder
1 cup chopped dates

1 cup chopped walnuts
1 cup cranberries, chopped
Grated rind of 2 oranges
2 eggs, beaten
¾ cup vegetable oil
1 cup buttermilk

Glaze:
¾ cup sugar

¾ cup orange juice

Mix first 5 ingredients together. Stir in dates, nuts, cranberries, and orange rind. Combine eggs with oil and buttermilk. Add to flour mixture. Bake in tube pan at 325° for 1 hour. Keep cake in pan on rack.

Heat sugar and orange juice until sugar dissolves. Pour over hot cake. Let sit 3 minutes. Remove from pan and let sit 24 hours.

Grocery List: 1 pkg. dates, 1 pkg. walnuts, 1 pkg. fresh cranberries, 2 oranges,
1 qt. buttermilk

Pantry Checklist: Flour, Sugar, Salt, Baking soda, Oil, Baking powder, Eggs

Applesauce Cake

½ cup shortening	1½ cups sugar	2 eggs
2 Tbsp. cocoa	1½ cups applesauce	½ tsp. cinnamon
½ tsp. cloves	½ tsp. nutmeg	½ tsp. allspice
1¼ tsp. baking powder	2 cups all-purpose flour	¾ tsp. salt
¾ cup raisins	¾ cup mixed fruit	¾ cup pecans

Cream together shortening and sugar. Add eggs, cocoa, applesauce, spices, and other ingredients. Bake in greased and floured bundt pan at 350° for 55 to 60 minutes.

Grocery List: 1 jar applesauce, 1 pkg. pecans, 1 pkg. mixed fruit, 1 box raisins

Pantry Checklist: Shortening, Cocoa, Flour, Sugar, Salt, Eggs, Baking powder, Cinnamon, Cloves, Nutmeg, Allspice

Toffee Bar Cake

2 cups all-purpose flour	2 cups brown sugar
½ cup butter	1 egg
1 cup buttermilk	1 tsp. baking soda
1 tsp. vanilla	½ cup pecans, chopped
6 English toffee bars, crushed	

Place flour, sugar, and butter in mixing bowl. Cut mixture to coarse crumb consistency using a pastry blender. Save 1 cup of mixture for topping. To remainder of mixture, add egg, buttermilk (to which soda has been added), and vanilla. Mix well and pour into a well-greased 9 x 13 pan. Sprinkle remaining crumbs and nuts on top. Sprinkle crushed toffee bars on top. Bake at 350° for 30 to 40 minutes. Serve with whipped topping.

Grocery List: 1 box brown sugar, 1 pkg. pecans, 6 toffee bars, 1 qt. buttermilk

Pantry Checklist: Flour, Egg, Baking soda, Vanilla, Butter

Note: Cut toffee bars with kitchen scissors; it's very easy.

Cold Oven Pound Cake

½ cup shortening   ½ cup margarine   3 cups sugar
1 cup milk   1 tsp. vanilla   3 cups all-purpose flour
5 eggs   1 tsp. baking powder   ⅛ tsp. salt

Cream margarine, shortening, and sugar until well mixed. Add eggs (one at a time) and beat until light and fluffy. Sift flour, baking powder and salt and add alternately with 1 cup milk. Add vanilla. Beat well. Pour into 3 greased, floured loaf pans and bake at 325° for 1 hour and 15 minutes. Start with cold oven. Do not open while baking.

Topping:
1 cup sugar   ¼ cup water
½ cup margarine   1 Tbsp. butternut flavoring

Mix in pan and bring to boil. Pour over hot cake in pan.

*G*rocery List: 5 lbs. sugar, 5 lbs. flour, 1 dozen eggs

*P*antry Checklist: Shortening, Margarine, Milk, Vanilla, Baking powder, Salt, Butternut flavoring

Kitchen Hint: Dip spoon or measuring cup in hot water before measuring shortening or butter; it will slide out easily without sticking.

7-Up Cake

3 cups sugar   1½ cups butter
5 eggs   3 cups flour
¾ cup 7-Up   2 Tbsp. lemon extract

Cream sugar and butter together until light and fluffy. Add eggs, one at a time, and beat well. Add flour alternately with 7-Up. Add lemon. Bake in a tube pan at 325° for 1 hour and 15 minutes.

*G*rocery List: 1 lb. butter, 1 dozen eggs, 7-Up

*P*antry Checklist: Lemon extract, Sugar, Flour

Chocolate Cake with White Frosting

(Michael's favorite cake)

Prepare 1 package Duncan Hines chocolate butter cake mix as directed and bake in 3 round cake pans.

Frosting for cake:
½ cup shortening
1 tsp. vanilla
Enough milk to mix

1 box powdered sugar
⅛ tsp. almond flavoring

Mix together and frost cooled cake. Stack layers.

Grocery List: 1 box Duncan Hines chocolate butter cake mix, 1 box powdered sugar

Pantry Checklist: Vanilla, Eggs, Margarine, Milk, Shortening, Almond flavoring

Brown Sugar Pound Cake

¾ cup shortening
1 lb. light brown sugar
5 egg yolks, well beaten
½ tsp. baking powder
1 cup pecans
5 egg whites, beaten

¾ cup butter
½ cup white sugar
3 cups all-purpose flour
1 cup milk
1 tsp. vanilla

Cream shortening, butter, and brown and white sugars until well mixed. Stir in beaten egg yolks. Sift flour with the baking powder and add alternately with milk to the above mixture. Add nuts and vanilla and fold in well-beaten egg whites. Bake in well-greased tube pan at 350° for 1 hour and 15 minutes.

Grocery List: 1 box light brown sugar, 1 pkg. pecans, 1 dozen eggs

Pantry Checklist: Sugar, Flour, Butter, Baking powder, Vanilla, Shortening, Milk

Kitchen Hint: A slice of soft bread placed inside a package of hardened brown sugar will soften it again in a couple of hours.

Fresh Apple Cake

2 cups all-purpose flour	2 cups sugar	¼ tsp. salt
2 tsp. cinnamon	2 tsp. baking soda	½ tsp. nutmeg
½ tsp. ginger	2 eggs	½ cup vegetable oil
4 cups apples, diced	1 cup chopped dates	1 cup chopped pecans

Combine dry ingredients. Add eggs and oil, then apples. Batter will be very stiff. Stir dates and nuts with 2 tablespoons flour and add to apple mixture. Spread batter in 3 round greased and floured cake pans. Bake at 350° for 40 minutes.
Let sit 5 minutes before removing from pans. Cool and frost with cream cheese frosting.

Cream Cheese Frosting:
1 pkg. (8 oz.) cream cheese	½ cup margarine
1 box powdered sugar	1 tsp. vanilla

Have all ingredients at room temperature. Combine and beat until smooth.

Grocery List: 4 to 6 apples, 1 pkg. pecans, 8 oz. cream cheese, 1 box powdered sugar, 1 pkg. dates

Pantry Checklist: Eggs, Oil, Flour, Sugar, Salt, Cinnamon, Baking soda, Vanilla, Margarine, Nutmeg, Ginger

Strawberry Cake

1 box white cake mix	¼ cup water	1 small box	1 box (10 oz.) frozen
4 eggs	¾ cup oil	strawberry gelatin	strawberries, thawed

Mix above ingredients with mixer and beat well. Spread in 3 greased round cake pans and bake at 350° for 20 to 30 minutes or until done.

Frosting:
1 box powdered sugar, sifted	½ cup margarine
1 pkg. (10 oz.) frozen strawberries, thawed	

Mix sugar and margarine until smooth. Add strawberries. Beat until smooth.

Grocery List: 1 white cake mix, 1 small strawberry gelatin, 2 pkgs. (10 oz.) frozen strawberries, 1 box powdered sugar

Pantry Checklist: Eggs, Oil, Margarine

Texas Chocolate Cake

2 cups all-purpose flour
½ cup shortening
1 tsp. baking soda
1 tsp. vanilla

2 cups sugar
4 Tbsp. cocoa
½ cup buttermilk

1 stick margarine
1 cup water
2 eggs (unbeaten)

Sift together flour and sugar. Bring to a boil the margarine, shortening, cocoa, and water; pour over flour-sugar mixture; add the soda and buttermilk and stir, then add eggs and vanilla and mix well. Grease and flour a 9 x 13 pan and bake at 350° for 30 minutes. Cool and then frost.

Frosting:
1 stick margarine
1 tsp. vanilla

6 Tbsp. buttermilk
1 box powdered sugar

4 Tbsp. cocoa
1 cup chopped pecans

Bring margarine, buttermilk, and cocoa to a boil. Remove from heat and add vanilla, sugar, and nuts. Spread over cake.

Grocery List: 1 box cocoa, 1 qt. buttermilk, 1 box powdered sugar, 1 pkg. pecans

Pantry Checklist: Flour, Margarine, Baking soda, Eggs, Sugar, Shortening, Vanilla

Pineapple-Orange Pudding Cake

1 box Duncan Hines
   yellow butter cake mix

1 can (11 oz.) mandarin
   oranges (not drained)

4 eggs
½ cup cooking oil

Mix all ingredients in mixer and blend well. Bake in 3 round greased cake pans at 350° for 18 to 20 minutes or until done.

Frosting:
1 carton (8 oz.) whipped topping   1 small box vanilla instant pudding (dry)
1 can (8¼ oz.) crushed pineapple (not drained)

While cake is baking, mix frosting ingredients and place in refrigerator. After cake is cool, spread frosting between layers and on top of cake.

Grocery List: 1 Duncan Hines yellow butter cake mix, 1 small can mandarin oranges, 1 (8 oz.) whipped topping, 1 small pkg. vanilla instant pudding, 1 small can crushed pineapple

Pantry Checklist: Eggs, Oil

Carrot Cake

4 eggs	2 cups sugar	1½ cups salad oil
2 cups self-rising flour	1 tsp. cinnamon	1 tsp. vanilla
¼ tsp. black walnut flavoring	1 cup shredded carrots	1 cup walnuts

Mix eggs, sugar, and oil. Add flour, cinnamon, vanilla, walnut flavoring, carrots, and walnuts. Bake in bundt pan at 350° for 1¼ hours. While cake is hot, spoon glaze over cake.

Glaze:

1 cup sugar	1 cup buttermilk
½ tsp. baking soda	1 tsp. Karo syrup

Bring the above ingredients to a boil (will be very foamy). Spoon over cake.

Grocery List: Carrots, 1 pkg. chopped walnuts, 1 bottle black walnut flavoring, 1 small bag self-rising flour, Buttermilk

Pantry Checklist: Eggs, Cinnamon, Oil, Vanilla, Sugar, Baking soda, Karo syrup

Lemon Apricot Cake

1 yellow cake mix	4 egg yolks
½ cup oil	1 cup apricot nectar
2 tsp. lemon juice	4 egg whites

Mix first 5 ingredients together; beat egg whites until stiff and fold into batter. Place in bundt pan and bake at 325° for 1 hour.

Glaze:

1½ cups powdered sugar	Juice and rind of 2 lemons

Heat sugar, juice, and rind until sugar is dissolved. Pour over warm cake.

Grocery List: 1 yellow cake mix, 2 lemons, 1 small can apricot nectar, 1 box powdered sugar

Pantry Checklist: Eggs, Oil

Italian Cream Cake

1 stick margarine	½ cup shortening	2 cups sugar
5 egg yolks	2 cups all-purpose flour	1 tsp. baking soda
½ tsp. salt	1 cup buttermilk	1 tsp. vanilla
1 cup pecans	1 cup flaked coconut	5 egg whites, beaten

Cream margarine, shortening, and sugar; add egg yolks and beat well. Sift flour, soda, and salt together and add alternately with the buttermilk (flour first and last). Add vanilla. Stir in nuts and coconut and fold in egg whites, which have been beaten to stand in peaks. Pour into 3 greased and floured round 9-inch cake pans. Bake at 350° for 25 minutes.

Icing:

1 pkg. (8 oz.) cream cheese (at room temperature)	1 tsp. vanilla
1 lb. box powdered sugar	½ cup butter or margarine

Mix all ingredients together. If too thick, add a tablespoon or so of milk.

Grocery List: 1 lb. margarine, 1 dozen eggs, 1 pkg. coconut, 1 pkg. pecans, 1 qt. buttermilk, 8 oz. cream cheese, 1 box powdered sugar

Pantry Checklist: Baking soda, Salt, Shortening, Flour, Sugar, Vanilla

Chocolate Pecan Coconut Cake

1 Swiss chocolate cake mix	¾ cup coconut	½ cup pecans

Prepare cake mix as directed and add coconut and pecans. Pour batter into 3 well-greased cake pans and bake at 350° for 15 to 18 minutes or until done.

Icing:

1 pkg. (8 oz.) cream cheese	1 tsp. vanilla
½ cup butter or margarine	1 box powdered sugar

Mix together well and frost cake.

Grocery List: 1 Swiss chocolate cake mix, 1 pkg. coconut, 1 pkg. pecans, 8 oz. cream cheese, 1 box powdered sugar

Pantry Checklist: Eggs, Oil, Vanilla, Margarine

Kate's Fruitcake

(Debbie's grandmother)

1 cup butter	3 cups sugar	10 eggs
1 lb. candied pineapple	1 lb. candied cherries	1 lb. pecans
4½ cups flour	2 tsp. baking powder	1 cup milk
2 cups coconut	1 cup orange juice	½ cup sugar

Cream butter and sugar well; add eggs and beat until creamy. Meanwhile mix fruit and nuts with 1 cup flour and set aside. Mix 3½ cups flour and baking powder into sugar-egg mixture, then add milk. Mix in fruit-flour mixture and add coconut. Bake in greased and floured tube pan at 275° for 2 hours. During last 30 minutes of baking, baste with the following: 1 cup orange juice and ½ cup sugar (boil until sugar is dissolved).

Grocery List: 1 dozen eggs, 1 lb. butter, 5 lbs. flour, 1 pkg. pecans, 1 pkg. coconut, 1 pkg. each candied pineapple and cherries, 1 qt. orange juice

Pantry Checklist: Baking powder, Sugar, Milk

Buttermilk Cake

1 cup butter	3 cups sugar	4 eggs
¼ tsp. baking soda	1 cup buttermilk	3 cups flour
1 tsp. vanilla	1 tsp. fresh lemon juice	1 cup pecans

Cream butter and sugar well; add eggs, 1 at a time, and beat until light and fluffy. Add soda to buttermilk. Alternately add flour and buttermilk mixture to the sugar-butter-egg mixture. Add vanilla and fresh lemon juice. Grease and flour tube pan; add 1 cup pecans on bottom of pan, then add cake batter. Bake at 325° for 1½ hours.

Grocery List: 1 lb. butter, 1 lemon, 1 qt. buttermilk, 1 lemon, 1 pkg. pecans

Pantry Checklist: Eggs, Baking soda, Vanilla, Sugar, Flour

Coconut Cake

1 box Duncan Hines yellow
    butter cake mix
Coconut

Rich's frozen whipped topping
    (purchase at wholesale grocer)

Prepare cake as directed and bake in 3 9-inch cake pans at 350° for 15 minutes (or until done). Cool. Ice the cake with the topping and then add coconut to each layer. Frost sides with whipped topping. This cake freezes well; otherwise keep in refrigerator.

Grocery List: 1 box yellow cake mix (Duncan Hines butter), 1 can Rich's frozen whipped topping

Pantry Checklist: Coconut, Butter, Eggs

Note: If you do not live near a wholesale grocer, a large container of frozen whipped topping will work in this recipe.

Photo: Dennis Sabo

Michael at a *Change Your World* Concert in 1993

Orange Date Nut Cake

1 cup butter	1¾ cups sugar	3 eggs
3 cups all-purpose flour	1½ tsp. salt	1½ tsp. baking soda
1 cup buttermilk	1 Tbsp. orange juice	1 cup dates, cut up
Grated rind of one orange	1 cup pecans, chopped	

Cream butter and sugar. Add eggs and beat until light and fluffy; sift flour, salt, and soda and add alternately with buttermilk. Add orange juice, then dates and nuts. Bake in greased and floured tube pan at 350° for 1 hour.

Sauce:
Grated rind of one orange   1 cup sugar
1 cup orange juice

Combine and bring to boil. Pour over hot cake.

Grocery List: 1 pkg. pecans, 1 qt. buttermilk, 1 qt. orange juice, 1 orange, 1 pkg. dates

Pantry Checklist: Sugar, Eggs, Flour, Baking soda, Salt, Butter

Brownie Trifle

1 pkg. fudge brownie mix	1 small box chocolate instant pudding
6 toffee bars, crushed	1 cup pecans, toasted
2 cartons (8 oz.) frozen whipped topping	

Prepare and bake brownie mix according to package directions. Prepare chocolate pudding mix; cool and mix with 8 ounces of whipped topping. Crumble brownies; divide into 3 portions and place one portion in bottom of trifle bowl, then ⅓ of chocolate mix, ⅓ of whipped topping, 2 crushed toffee bars, and ⅓ cup toasted pecans. Repeat layers two more times. Cover and chill for several hours before serving.

Grocery List: 1 pkg. fudge brownie mix, 1 small box chocolate instant pudding, 6 toffee bars, 2 cartons (8 oz.) frozen whipped topping, 1 small pkg. pecans

Pantry Checklist: Milk

Angel Pie

12 large egg whites, separated
3 cups sugar
1½ Tbsp. vanilla

1½ tsp. cream of tartar
½ tsp. salt

Beat egg whites and cream of tartar until stiff; gradually add sugar, salt, and vanilla. Place mixture in 2 greased glass 9 x 13 baking dishes and bake at 250° for 1 hour. Cool.

Filling:
12 egg yolks
5 Tbsp. hot water
Grated rind of 1 lemon

¾ cup sugar
Juice of 2 lemons
2 pts. whipping cream

Combine ingredients in double boiler and cook until thick. After mixture cools, place thin layer on top of each dish of meringue. Whip 1 pint whipping cream and place on top of lemon sauce. Refrigerate overnight.

Grocery List: 1 dozen eggs, 2 lemons, 2 pts. whipping cream

Pantry Checklist: Cream of tartar, Sugar, Salt, Vanilla

Pumpkin Crunch

1 pkg. Duncan Hines Yellow
   Moist Deluxe cake mix
3 eggs, beaten
1 tsp. pumpkin pie spice
1 cup pecans

1 can (16 oz.) pumpkin
1 can (12 oz.) evaporated milk
1½ cups sugar
½ tsp. salt
1 cup butter, melted

Grease bottom of 9 x 13 dish. Combine and mix pumpkin, milk, eggs, sugar, spice, and salt. Pour into dish and sprinkle dry cake mix evenly over mixture. Top with pecans; drizzle with butter. Bake at 350° for 50 to 55 minutes until golden brown. Cool completely before serving. Serve with whipped topping.

Grocery List: 1 Duncan Hines yellow cake mix, 1 can (16 oz.) pumpkin, 1 pkg. pecans, 1 can evaporated milk, 1 small container whipped topping

Pantry Checklist: Sugar, Salt, Pumpkin pie spice, Butter, Eggs

Buttercreams

1 lb. powdered sugar
1 Tbsp. milk or more
1 box semisweet baking chocolate

½ cup butter (room temperature)
1 tsp. vanilla
Paraffin

Mix powdered sugar, butter, milk, and vanilla together with mixer (using dough hook) or by hand. Roll into balls and place on foil-lined cookie sheet. In double boiler, melt 5 squares semisweet chocolate and 1 square paraffin (size equal to 1 chocolate square or more if needed). Dip candy mixture in chocolate and place on foil-lined pan. Store in cool place or refrigerator.

Grocery List: 1 box powdered sugar, 1 lb. butter, paraffin, 1 box semisweet baking chocolate

Pantry Checklist: Milk, Vanilla

Note: You can add peanut butter, coconut, chopped cherries, or pecans to this creamy candy.

Banana Pudding

¾ cup sugar
½ tsp. salt
2 egg yolks, beaten
1 tsp. vanilla
Vanilla wafers

3 Tbsp. cornstarch
2 cups milk
2 tsp. butter
4 bananas, sliced

Mix sugar, cornstarch, and salt in saucepan. Gradually stir in milk. Cook over medium heat, stirring constantly, until mixture begins to thicken. Remove from heat and gradually stir 1 cup of hot mixture into egg yolks. Mix well and return to mixture in saucepan. Continue cooking until mixture is thickened. Remove from heat and blend in butter and vanilla.

Layer pudding with bananas and vanilla wafers. Chill thoroughly. Garnish with whipped cream.

Grocery List: 1 dozen eggs, 4 bananas, 1 box vanilla wafers

Pantry Checklist: Sugar, Cornstarch, Butter, Vanilla, Salt, Milk, Eggs

Banana Trifle

1⅓ cups sugar
¾ cup flour
½ tsp. salt
2 Tbsp. rum extract
5 bananas, sliced
2 cups whipping cream

8 egg yolks, beaten
1 Tbsp. vanilla
4 cups milk
1 pkg. (12 oz.) vanilla wafers
6 English toffee candy bars, crushed
2 Tbsp. powdered sugar

Combine first 3 ingredients in a large pan; whisk in milk. Bring to a boil over medium heat, stirring constantly. Remove mixture from heat. Beat egg yolks until thick and pale. Gradually stir about ¼ of hot mixture into yolks; add to the remaining hot mixture, stirring constantly. Continue stirring and cooking for 1 minute. Stir in vanilla and rum extract.

Layer ⅓ of wafers in the bottom of a trifle dish. Top with ⅓ of banana. Spoon ⅓ of custard over bananas, and sprinkle with ⅓ cup of crushed candy bar. Repeat procedure twice.

Beat whipping cream at medium speed with an electric mixer until it begins to thicken; gradually add powdered sugar, beating until soft peaks form. Spread whipped cream over trifle and sprinkle with remaining crushed candy bar. Cover and chill.

Grocery List: 1 dozen eggs, 1 box vanilla wafers, 5 bananas, 6 English toffee candy bars, 2 pts. whipping cream, rum extract

Pantry Checklist: Sugar, Flour, Milk, Powdered sugar, Vanilla

Strawberry Shortcake

⅓ cup shortening
1½ cups all-purpose flour
¼ tsp. baking soda

¼ cup sugar
1 tsp. baking powder
½ cup sour cream

1 egg
½ tsp. salt
1 qt. fresh strawberries

Mix shortening, sugar, and egg; mix until smooth and add dry ingredients alternately with sour cream. Stir just until mixed. Using a ⅓ measuring cup, drop onto greased cookie sheet. Bake at 350° for 12 to 15 minutes until brown. When cool, split open and serve with fresh strawberries and whipped topping.

Grocery List: 1 pt. sour cream, 1 pt. whipped topping, 1 qt. fresh strawberries

Pantry Checklist: Shortening, Flour, Sugar, Egg, Baking powder, Salt, Baking soda

Rainbow Sherbet Dessert

2 cups whipping cream
1 tsp. vanilla
¾ cup chopped pecans, toasted
2½ cups raspberry sherbet, softened
2½ cups orange sherbet, softened

3 Tbsp. powdered sugar
12 coconut macaroons, crushed
 and toasted
2½ cups lime sherbet, softened
Strawberry halves

Whip cream until frothy; add sugar and vanilla, beating until soft peaks form. Fold in macaroons and pecans. Spread half of mixture in a 9-inch springform pan; freeze. Spread a layer of each sherbet over whipped cream mixture, allowing each layer to freeze before spreading next layer. Top with remaining whipped cream mixture. Cover and freeze. Remove from pan and place on serving plate. Garnish with strawberries.

Grocery List: 2 pt. whipping cream, 1 pkg. coconut macaroons, ½ gallon each raspberry, lime, orange sherbet, 1 pt. fresh strawberries, 1 small pkg. pecans

Pantry Checklist: Powdered sugar, Vanilla

Kitchen Hint: To soften ice cream for easy serving, warm in microwave oven for 10 to 15 seconds, let stand two or three minutes, and serve.

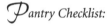

Chocolate-Dipped Butterhorns

¼ cup creamy peanut butter
2 cups corn snacks (Bugles)

3 squares (2 oz. each) chocolate
 candy coating, melted

Spoon peanut butter into a small plastic bag, snip a small hole in corner of bag, and squeeze a small amount of peanut butter into each corn snack. Dip each into chocolate coating and place on waxed paper to dry.

Grocery List: 1 box Bugles, 1 pkg. chocolate coating

Pantry Checklist: Peanut butter

Cheesecake

(Michael's favorite)

3 pkgs. (8 oz.) cream cheese	1 cup sugar
3 eggs	½ tsp. vanilla
1 carton (16 oz.) sour cream	3 Tbsp. sugar
½ tsp. vanilla	

Beat cream cheese at high speed with electric mixer until light and fluffy; gradually add 1 cup sugar, beating well. Add eggs, one at a time, beating well after each addition. Stir in vanilla. Pour into prepared crust. (See crust recipes on pages 181-182.) Bake at 375° for 35 minutes or until cheesecake is set.

Beat sour cream at medium speed for 2 minutes. Add 3 tablespoons sugar and ½ tsp. vanilla; beat an additional 1 minute. Spread over cheesecake and bake at 500° for 5 minutes. Let cool to room temperature on a wire rack; chill at least 8 hours. Serve with fresh strawberries, raspberry glaze, or drizzle with chocolate sauce.

Grocery List: 3 pkgs. (8 oz.) cream cheese, 1 container (16 oz.) sour cream

Pantry Checklist: Eggs, Sugar, Vanilla

Nutty Crust

½ cup butter	½ cup brown sugar, firmly packed
1 cup flour	½ cup finely chopped pecans

Cream butter with brown sugar in small bowl. Add flour and nuts. Mix until crumbly. Press into bottom of pan. Bake at 350° for 12 to 15 minutes.

Grocery List: 1 box brown sugar, 1 small pkg. pecans

Pantry Checklist: Butter, Flour

Lemon Peel Crust

1 cup flour
½ cup sugar
1 tsp. grated lemon peel

½ cup butter
1 egg yolk, beaten
½ tsp. vanilla

Mix first 3 ingredients and cut in butter. Add egg and vanilla and blend well. Pat ⅓ of dough in bottom of springform pan and bake at 400° about 6 minutes. Spread rest of dough on sides of pan. Add cheesecake mixture and finish baking.

Grocery List: 1 lemon

Pantry Checklist: Sugar, Butter, Flour, Eggs

Graham Cracker Crust

1⅔ cups graham cracker crumbs
¼ cup sugar

¼ cup plus 3 Tbsp. butter or
    margarine, melted

Combine all ingredients, mixing well. Firmly press mixture evenly over bottom and sides of springform pan or pie plate.

Grocery List: 1 box graham cracker crumbs

Pantry Checklist: Butter, Sugar

Punch Bowl Cake

1 box Duncan Hines yellow butter cake mix (bake 2 layers; I freeze extra layer)
1 qt. fresh strawberries, sliced and sweetened with 8-10 packets artificial
    sweetener or ½ cup sugar
1 large can crushed pineapple (in its own juice)
2 pkgs. (4 oz. each) vanilla instant pudding, prepared
2 cartons (8 oz.) whipped topping
1 pt. fresh blueberries

Bake cake as directed. (Pour batter into 2 round cake pans.) After cake has cooled,
tear 1 layer into pieces and place in bottom of punch bowl, then layer fruit,
pudding, and whipped topping as listed above. Repeat twice. Chill in refrigerator.
Garnish with kiwifruit just before serving.

Grocery List: 1 Duncan Hines yellow butter cake mix, 1 qt. fresh strawberries,
1 large can crushed pineapple, 1 pt. blueberries, 2 small pkgs. vanilla
instant pudding, 2 cartons (8 oz.) whipped topping, Kiwifruit

Hot Fudge Sauce

(Michael likes this sauce on vanilla ice cream.)

1 can Hershey's chocolate syrup
1½ tsp. vanilla
1 can sweetened condensed milk

1 stick butter
¼ tsp. salt

Heat chocolate syrup and butter in heavy pan over medium heat until it nearly
comes to a rolling boil. Add vanilla, salt, and then condensed milk, stirring very
rapidly as it is poured in. Immediately reduce heat to low and continue to stir
constantly until well emulsified. Do not remove from low temperature for several
minutes. You will notice it begin to get thick and creamy. Remove from heat and
stir occasionally. Serve while warm over ice cream.

Grocery List: 1 can condensed milk, 1 can Hershey's chocolate syrup

Pantry Checklist: Vanilla, Salt, Butter

Desserts

Emily puts red and green sprinkles on
Mimi's sugar cookies.

Ryan and Mary Claire, Kimberly's daughter,
enjoy a tea party on our back deck.

Anna and Emily with a special snack.

Mimi and her "angels"—Mary Claire, Caroline,
Whitney, and Emily—make Christmas cookies.

Cooking with the Kids

One of my greatest blessings is cooking with the grandkids. Of course, the most popular recipes are cookies. All of the children love sugar (much to their mothers' disappointment). When Emily cooks, more sprinkles go in her mouth than on the cookies!

This is not just a holiday event. We often bake cookies for tea parties and snacks. I hope to bequeath my love of cooking and special family mealtimes to my grandchildren, and cooking with them is just plain fun. (Maybe they'll remember Mimi when they bake with their own children.)

Sugar Cookies

½ cup shortening
1 egg
½ tsp. grated orange peel
¼ tsp. salt
2 to 3 Tbsp. milk

¾ cup sugar
½ tsp. vanilla
2 cups all-purpose flour
½ tsp. baking powder
1 cup powdered sugar

Cream shortening and sugar thoroughly. Add egg and beat well. Add vanilla and grated orange peel. Add dry ingredients alternately with milk and mix thoroughly. You can either roll out the cookies or use a cookie press. Bake at 375° for 10 to 12 minutes or until brown. *Yield:* 5 dozen.

Icing: Mix 1 cup powdered sugar with just enough water to make thin icing. Ice and sprinkle with colored sugar.

Grocery List: 1 orange, 1 box powdered sugar

Pantry Checklist: Shortening, Sugar, Egg, Vanilla, Flour, Salt, Baking powder

Raspberry Thumbprint Cookies

⅔ cup sugar
2 cups flour

1 cup butter
½ cup raspberry jam

½ tsp. vanilla

Glaze:
1 cup powdered sugar   1½ tsp. vanilla   2 to 3 tsp. water

Combine sugar, butter, and vanilla. Beat at medium speed until creamy. Reduce speed to low; add flour. Beat until well mixed. Cover and chill dough at least 1 hour. Shape dough into 1-inch balls. Place 2 inches apart on cookie sheet. With thumb, make indentation in center of each cookie. Fill each indentation with about ¼ tsp. jam. Bake at 350° for 14 to 18 minutes or until edges are lightly browned. Let stand 1 minute; remove from cookie sheet. Cool completely. Meanwhile, in small bowl with wire whisk, stir together all glaze ingredients until smooth. Drizzle over cookies. *Yield:* 3½ dozen cookies.

Grocery List: 1 jar raspberry jam

Pantry Checklist: Sugar, Butter, Vanilla, Flour, Powdered sugar

Desserts

Nan's Peanut Butter Cookies

1 cup shortening	½ tsp. salt	1 tsp. baking soda
1 cup peanut butter	1 cup sugar	1 cup brown sugar
2 eggs, well beaten	2 cups all-purpose flour	

Combine shortening, salt, soda, and peanut butter and mix well. Add white and brown sugars and cream thoroughly. Add eggs and mix well; then add flour and blend. Drop by teaspoonfuls onto greased baking sheet; press cookies lightly with fork to flatten. Bake at 350° for 10 minutes or until brown. *Yield:* 5 dozen.

Grocery List: 1 can shortening, 1 small jar peanut butter

Pantry Checklist: Salt, Baking soda, White and brown sugars, Flour, Eggs

White Chocolate Chip Nut Cookies

1 cup butter, softened	2 eggs
2 tsp. vanilla	1 cup brown sugar
½ cup white sugar	2¼ cups cake flour
1 tsp. salt	1 tsp. baking soda
2 cups white chocolate chips	1 cup macadamia nuts

Cream butter; add eggs, vanilla and sugars. Combine dry ingredients and add to creamed mixture. Add chips and nuts. Drop by teaspoonfuls onto lightly greased cookie sheet. Bake at 325° for 12 minutes or until golden brown. Cool and remove to wire rack. *Yield:* 5 dozen.

Grocery List: 1 lb. butter, 1 box brown sugar, 1 box cake flour, 1 pkg. white chocolate chips, 1 pkg. macadamia nuts

Pantry Checklist: Eggs, Sugar, Vanilla, Salt, Baking soda

Orange Balls

1 box vanilla wafers, crushed
1 can (6 oz.) frozen orange juice
1 stick butter
1 cup chopped dates

½ cup chopped pecans
1 box powdered sugar
Coconut

Mix first 5 ingredients together well and shape into small balls; roll in powdered sugar and coconut, and freeze.

Grocery List: 1 box vanilla wafers, 1 pkg. dates, 6 oz. frozen orange juice, 1 pkg. pecans, 1 box powdered sugar, 1 pkg. coconut

Pantry Checklist: Butter

Kitchen Hint: Save time by measuring all ingredients before preparing a recipe.

Pecan Date Dip

1 pkg. (8 oz.) cream cheese
½ cup chopped pecans, toasted
½ cup chopped dates

⅛ tsp. ginger
Butter cookies

Mix first 4 ingredients together well. Serve with butter cookies.

Grocery List: 8 oz. cream cheese, 1 pkg. chopped dates, 1 small pkg. pecans, 1 pkg. butter cookies

Pantry Checklist: Ginger

Apple Crisp

4 cups Granny Smith apples, diced
2 Tbsp. lemon juice
1 cup white or brown sugar
½ cup butter

½ cup water
¾ cup flour
1 tsp. cinnamon
½ cup chopped pecans

Arrange apples in buttered baking dish. Combine water and lemon juice and pour over apples. Stir flour, sugar, cinnamon, and butter with fork. Place this mixture on top of apples, then pecans. Bake at 350° about 30 minutes or until apples are tender and crust is brown. Serve warm with vanilla ice cream.

Grocery List: 6 Granny Smith apples, 1 small pkg. pecans, Vanilla ice cream

Pantry Checklist: Sugar, Cinnamon, Flour, Butter, Lemon juice

Millionaire Tarts

1 cup golden raisins
3 eggs, beaten
2 Tbsp. butter
1 tsp. cinnamon
½ tsp. nutmeg
Whipping cream

6 Tbsp. water
1½ cup sugar
1 Tbsp. vinegar
¼ tsp. allspice
1 cup chopped pecans
Tart shells

Boil raisins in water for 5 minutes. Add remaining ingredients, except nuts and whipping cream, and cook until thick. Cool; stir in nuts. Fill tart shells and top with whipping cream.

Grocery List: 1 box golden raisins, 1 pkg. pecans, 1 pt. whipping cream, Tart shells

Pantry Checklist: Eggs, Sugar, Butter, Vinegar, Cinnamon, Allspice, Nutmeg

Desserts

Banana Royale

3 ripe bananas, sliced lengthwise
½ cup butter, melted
½ cup golden raisins

1 cup brown sugar
1 Tbsp. brandy extract
½ cup chopped pecans

Preheat oven to 325°. Spray a shallow casserole dish with cooking spray. Cover bottom with layer of bananas. Mix brown sugar, melted butter, and brandy extract; sprinkle half of mixture on bananas. Add half of raisins and pecans. Repeat layers. Bake for 30 to 40 minutes.

Grocery List: 3 bananas, 1 box golden raisins, 1 pkg. pecans

Pantry Checklist: Brown sugar, Butter, Brandy extract

Blackberry Cobbler

3 cups fresh blackberries or 2 pkgs.
   (16 oz. each) frozen blackberries, thawed
1 Tbsp. lemon juice
2 Tbsp. margarine or butter

¾ cup sugar
3 Tbsp. flour
1 cup water
Crust (recipe follows)

Spread berries in a lightly greased 2-quart baking dish. Combine sugar and flour; stir in water and lemon juice. Pour mixture over berries, and bake at 425° for 15 minutes. Place crust over hot berries; brush with butter. Bake at 425° for 20 to 30 minutes or until crust is golden brown. Serve warm with ice cream, if desired.

Crust:
1¾ cups flour
2 tsp. baking powder
¾ tsp. salt
2 to 3 Tbsp. sugar

¼ cup shortening
¼ cup plus 3 Tbsp. milk
¼ cup plus 2 Tbsp. buttermilk

Pulse first 5 ingredients in food processor. Add milk and buttermilk. Mix well and roll out dough on floured surface. Cut dough to fit baking dish.

Grocery List: 2 large pkgs. frozen blackberries or 2 pts. fresh berries, Buttermilk

Pantry Checklist: Sugar, Flour, Margarine, Baking powder, Salt, Shortening, Lemon juice, Milk

Cornflake Cookies

1 cup margarine	1 cup butter	1¼ cups sugar
4 cups flour	1½ tsp. vanilla	1 cup chopped pecans
3 cups cornflakes		

Cream margarine and butter. Add rest of ingredients. Mix well; dough will be very thick. Do not worry if cornflakes crumble. Drop by teaspoonfuls onto ungreased cookie sheet. Flatten with fork. Bake at 350° for 12 to 15 minutes. *Yield:* 5 dozen.

Grocery List: 1 box cornflakes, 5 lbs. flour, 1 pkg. pecans

Pantry Checklist: Margarine, Butter, Sugar, Vanilla

Bread Pudding

½ lb. French bread	¼ cup pecans, toasted	1 cup raisins
¼ cup butter, melted		

Custard Mix:

8 large eggs	1 tsp. salt	2 cups sugar
1 tsp. vanilla	5½ cups milk	

Blend eggs, salt, and sugar lightly with wire whisk. Add vanilla and milk; blend well.
   Break French bread into medium pieces. Add pecans, raisins, and melted butter. Arrange in large greased baking pan. Pour custard mix over bread pieces. Bake (with dish placed in pan or water) at 350° for 20 to 25 minutes. Test with knife.

Note: For custard to bake properly, you must create this double-boiler effect. Plan size of pan accordingly.

Brandy Sauce:

½ cup butter	1 cup sugar	½ can evaporated milk
2 Tbsp. brandy extract		

Combine butter, sugar, and half-and-half in a heavy saucepan; cook over medium heat until sugar dissolves. Bring to a boil; reduce heat and simmer 5 minutes. Remove from heat. Let cool and add brandy extract.

Grocery List: 1 loaf French bread, ½ gallon milk, 1 can evaporated milk, 1 bottle brandy extract, 1 pkg. pecans, 1 pkg. raisins, 1 dozen eggs

Pantry Checklist: Butter, Sugar, Vanilla, Salt

Cream Puffs

½ cup butter

1 cup sifted all-purpose flour

4 eggs

1 cup boiling water

¼ tsp. salt

Melt butter in boiling water; add flour and salt. Cook and stir vigorously until mixture forms a ball. Remove from heat and cool slightly. Add eggs, 1 at a time, beating hard after each addition until mixture is smooth.

Form cream puffs (the size you prefer) on an ungreased cookie sheet. Bake at 400° for 15 minutes, then reduce heat to 325° and cook for 25 minutes. Cool on wire rack.

Filling:

1 cup sugar

2½ cups milk

2 Tbsp. butter

Dash of salt

3 egg yolks

4½ Tbsp. cornstarch

1 tsp. vanilla

Mix sugar, salt, and cornstarch. Add milk gradually and cook over medium heat until mixture starts to thicken. Beat egg yolks and add to hot mixture. Cook until thick. Add vanilla and butter. Fill puffs when mixture cools. Drizzle a chocolate glaze over the top (melt chocolate square with 1 tablespoon milk and enough powdered sugar to make glaze).

Grocery List: 1 qt. milk, 1 box semisweet baking chocolate

Pantry Checklist: Sugar, Cornstarch, Salt, Vanilla, Flour, Butter, Eggs, Powdered sugar

Note: These cream puffs can be made very small for cocktail parties and filled with any filling you desire. If making small puffs, bake at 400° for 10 minutes, then at 325° for 20 minutes. Watch them carefully so they don't get too brown.

Strawberry Squares

1 cup flour
½ cup pecans, chopped

¼ cup brown sugar
½ cup margarine

Mix ingredients and spread evenly in shallow pan. Bake at 350° for 20 minutes, stirring occasionally. Sprinkle ⅔ of the crumbs in a 13 x 9 x 2 pan. Reserve the remainder for topping.

Filling:

1 cup whipping cream   2 egg whites
1 pkg. (10 oz.) frozen strawberries, partially thawed

⅔ cup sugar
2 tsp. lemon juice

Whip cream. Using clean beaters and another bowl, combine egg whites, sugar, berries, and lemon juice. Beat at high speed to stiff peaks, about 10 minutes. Fold in cream. Place on top of crumbs and top with remaining crumbs. Freeze at least 6 hours.

Grocery List: 1 box brown sugar, 1 pkg. pecans, 1 pkg. (10 oz.) frozen strawberries, 1 pt. whipping cream

Pantry Checklist: Flour, Margarine, Eggs, Sugar, Lemon juice

Frozen Orange Dessert

60 round butter cookies,
  crushed (3 cups)
½ cup butter, melted
¼ cup sugar
1 carton (8 oz.) whipped topping

1 can (14 oz.) sweetened
  condensed milk
1 can (6 oz.) frozen orange juice
  concentrate, thawed and undiluted
2 cans (11 oz. each) cans mandarin
  oranges, drained

Combine first 3 ingredients; set aside ¾ cup crumbs. Press remaining crumb mixture into an ungreased 9 x 13 baking dish. Combine condensed milk and orange juice; fold in whipped topping and oranges. Spoon over cooled crust and sprinkle reserved crumb mixture on top. Cover and freeze.

Grocery List: 1 pkg. butter cookies, 1 can condensed milk, 6 oz. frozen orange juice, 8 oz. whipped topping, 2 cans (11 oz. each) mandarin oranges

Pantry Checklist: Butter, Sugar

Meringue Shells

12 egg whites   2½ cups sugar   2 tsp. vanilla extract

Beat egg whites until stiff, gradually adding small amounts of sugar. Add vanilla extract and mix. Spray cooking spray on nonstick cookie sheet. Scoop meringue mixture in small mounds onto cookie sheet. Make an indentation with back of spoon for filling. Bake at 250° for 45 minutes; turn off oven and let cool for 30 minutes. These keep well in a tightly closed container. If shells become tacky in humid weather, bake at 150° for 10 minutes to dry them out.

Grocery List: 1 dozen eggs, 1 lb. sugar

Pantry Checklist: Vanilla, Cooking spray

Note: These can be made large or small. For party occasions, make small ones and top with whipped topping and a fresh strawberry half, kiwi slice, or blueberries.

Lime Fluff Cheesecake

1 pkg. (3 oz) lime gelatin   1 cup boiling water
1½ pkg. cream cheese (12 oz.)   1 cup powdered sugar
1 tsp. vanilla   1 carton (8 oz.) whipped topping
1 graham cracker crust

Dissolve gelatin in boiling water, stirring well; set aside to cool. Blend cream cheese, powdered sugar, and vanilla with electric mixer, beating until smooth. Add cooled gelatin and beat well. Fold in whipped topping. Pour into graham cracker crust and chill.

Grocery List: 1 small lime gelatin, 8 oz. whipped topping, 2 pkgs. (8 oz. each) cream cheese, 1 graham cracker crust

Pantry Checklist: Powdered sugar, Vanilla

Low-fat, sugar-free version: Use sugar-free gelatin, 8 pkgs. artificial sweetener (or more if needed), and low-fat whipped topping.

Index of Recipes

Index

197

Desserts

About the Author

Barbara Smith's priorities are her faith in God, her family, and friends. She believes it is very important to make family meals a special time of eating and sharing together. Barbara owned a catering business in West Virginia for thirteen years.

She and her husband, Paul, have two children—Kimberly Bennett and Michael W. Smith—and eight grandchildren. They reside in Franklin, Tennessee.

Photo: Alden Lockridge

Paul and Barbara Smith with their grandchildren
(left to right)—Ryan, Emily, Whitney, Mary Claire, Tyler, Caroline, and Anna. (Not shown: Sarah Kate Bennett)